SAXON SERIES IN ENGLISH AS A SECOND LANGUAGE

GRANT TAYLOR, Consulting Editor

LEARNING

AMERICAN

ENGLISH

GRAMMAR VOCABULARY IDIOMS

By GRANT TAYLOR, Formerly: Associate Professor of English; Director, American Language Institute, Division of General Education, New York University; Assistant Director, Foreign Student Center, New York University; Lecturer in English, Columbia University; Associate Editor, Thorndike-Barnhart Comprehensive Desk Dictionary.

McGRAW-HILL BOOK COMPANY

NEW YORK   LONDON   SYDNEY   TORONTO

SAXON SERIES IN ENGLISH AS A SECOND LANGUAGE

GRANT TAYLOR, Consulting Editor

LEARNING AMERICAN ENGLISH
MASTERING AMERICAN ENGLISH
PRACTICING AMERICAN ENGLISH
AMERICAN ENGLISH READER
MODERN ENGLISH ESSAYS
ADVANCED ENGLISH EXERCISES
MODERN SPOKEN ENGLISH
MODERN ENGLISH WORKBOOK
INDEX TO MODERN ENGLISH
AMERICAN READINGS
READING AMERICAN HISTORY
MASTERING SPOKEN ENGLISH I

LEARNING AMERICAN ENGLISH

The United States Library of Congress Catalog Card Number 56-9986.
ISBN 07-069241-2

15 EBEB 7 6 5 4 3

Preface

Learning American English was planned and written to meet the needs of adult students at the beginning and intermediate stages of learning English as a second language. As designed, the text is intended to be functional for either oral or written classroom work or home use. In developing the present text, the author has attempted to point up the need for [1] a good control over fundamentals and [2] a descriptive (or "realistic") approach to English.

The first objective is, more precisely, a knowledge of the basic language materials sufficient to enable the learner to use and understand them almost automatically. This knowledge is achieved through a logical and simplified presentation of grammar and structure, and an emphasis on constant practice with the most common elements of the language. In line with this approach, the scope of Learning American English has been limited to those features of English which occur most frequently and which, once mastered, equip the student for fruitful advanced study. The large number of exercises and drills in the text should accommodate many hours of both class and home practice.

A descriptive approach to English is one which stresses the forms which are in constant use by the majority of native speakers of English. Therefore, "correctness" is not determined by rules or tradition but by actual usage. The English thus described in the present text is the informal spoken language used by the majority of native American speakers.

The basic materials included in Learning American English have been divided into seventeen lessons, each followed by cumulative exercises. These materials are largely self-explanatory. Simplified box diagrams and numerous examples throughout make lengthy explanations unnecessary. Where explanations do occur, the language used in the explanations does not exceed that covered in the text up to that point. This means that students, if necessary, can go through the text with the aid of only a dictionary. At the rate of four to five class hours per week, intermediate students should be able to complete the text in the course of the usual semester.   With an equal number of hours available, beginning students should devote two semesters to the same work.

To meet the vocabulary demands of the intermediate student, the total number of vocabulary items included exceeds 1500.   However, beginning students should perhaps limit themselves to only the basic vocabulary — the 550 words which occur more than three times.   In selecting the basic vocabulary items, The Teacher's Word Book of 30,000 Words (E. L. Thorndike and Irving Lorge, N. Y., 1944) and the "K. L. M. List" in The History and Principles of Vocabulary Control (Herman Bongers, Holland, 1954) were used as principal sources of reference.

The author would like to express his indebtedness to Professors Anders Orbeck and John N. Winburne of Michigan State University for their generous encouragement and guidance. The author also wishes to thank Dr. Thomas L. Crowell of Columbia University for his many valuable suggestions and criticisms while this text was still in formative stages.

G. E. T.

New York, 1954

NOTE TO THE SECOND EDITION

The enthusiastic reception of Learning American English both in the United States and abroad has been very gratifying to me. I wish to thank the numerous teachers of English as a second language who have offered suggestions and useful comments, many of which have been incorporated in the second edition. Those teachers who have asked me about an appropriate text to use upon completion of Learning American English may wish to become acquainted with Mastering American English, an exercise book for intermediate and advanced students recently published by Saxon Press.

G. E. T.

New York, 1956

iv

Contents

LESSON ONE
1

1A The plural forms of nouns   1B The plural forms of irregular nouns   1C The definite and indefinite articles   1D Adjectives with nouns   1E The subject pronouns   1F The verb be   1G Statements, questions, and negatives   1H Contractions with be

LESSON TWO
10

2A The simple present tense   2B The simple present tense of do and have   2C Statements, questions, and negatives   2D The words this and these, that and those   2E Contractions with do and that   2F The prepositions in and on   2G Idioms

LESSON THREE
23

3A The continuous present tense   3B Statements, questions, and negatives   3C The two present tenses   3D Questions with the word what   3E The expressions there is and there are   3F The prepositions to and from   3G Idioms

LESSON FOUR
34

4A Summary of the present tenses   4B Short answers (I)   4C The word what with the two present tenses   4D The imperative forms   4E Polite forms   4F Suggestions with let's   4G The preposition of   4H Idioms

LESSON FIVE
46

5A The object pronouns   5B The object pronouns following verbs   5C The object pronouns after prepositions   5D The words much and many, a little and a few   5E The expressions a lot of and lots of   5F The words very and too   5G The words some and any   5H Frequency words   5J Idioms

LESSON SIX 59

6A The past tense of be 6B Statements, questions, and negatives 6C The past tense of regular verbs 6D Spelling the past tense forms of regular verbs 6E Statements, questions, and negatives 6F Contractions with was, were, and did 6G Time expressions with the past tense 6H The prepositions by and with 6H Idioms

LESSON SEVEN 70

7A The past tense of irregular verbs 7B Statements, questions, and negatives 7C The irregular verbs (part one) 7D In, on, and at in expressions of place 7E Direct and indirect objects 7F Idioms

LESSON EIGHT 81

8A The irregular verbs (part two) 8B The possessive forms of nouns 8C The possessive adjectives 8D The possessive pronouns 8E The preposition of 8F Idioms

LESSON NINE 93

9A Summary of the possessive forms 9B The future tense with will 9C Statements, questions, and negatives 9D Contractions with will 9E In, on, and at in expressions of time (part two) 9F Idioms

LESSON TEN 103

10A Expressions of time (part two) 10B Expressions of time (part three) 10C Future substitutes: be + going to 10D Future substitutes: the present tenses 10F Short answers (II) 10G The prepositions in, for, by, and until 10H Idioms

LESSON ELEVEN 114

11A The interrogative words where, when, and why 11B The interrogative word how 11C The interrogative words whose, which, and what 11D The interrogative words who and whom 11E The expressions what...for and how come 11F The expressions how about and what about 11G Contractions with the interrogative words 11H The indefinite one and you 11J The preposition out of

LESSON TWELVE   127

12A The present perfect tense 12B Statements, questions, and negatives 12C Have + got in place of have 12D The third form of irregular verbs 12E Contractions with have and has 12F The prepositions since and for 12G Idioms

LESSON THIRTEEN   139

13A The past tense and the present perfect tense 13B Negative questions 13C Negative questions with why 13D Answer presuming questions 13E The preposition for 13F Words with allied prepositions (part one)

LESSON FOURTEEN   152

14A The words no and not 14B The expressions still, any more, and any longer 14C The words already and yet 14D The words also, too, and either 14E Short additions with too and either 14F Words with allied prepositions (part two)

LESSON FIFTEEN   165

15A Word order: words before nouns 15B Word order: the word enough 15C Word order: the words something, anything, etc. 15D Word order: measurements 15E Word order: objects, place, manner, and time 15F Strong exclamations with what and how 15G Words with allied prepositions (part three)

LESSON SIXTEEN   181

16A The comparative and superlative forms 16B Spelling the comparative and superlative forms 16C Words with irregular comparatives and superlatives 16D Comparisons with as...as 16E General comparisons 16F The words same and different in comparisons 16G The expression one of with the superlative 16H Idioms

LESSON SEVENTEEN   193

17A The passive forms of verbs 17B Statements, questions, and negatives 17C The infinitive after certain verbs 17D The infinitive to show purpose 17E The gerund after certain verbs 17F The gerund after prepositions 17G The infinitive or gerund after certain verbs 17H Idioms

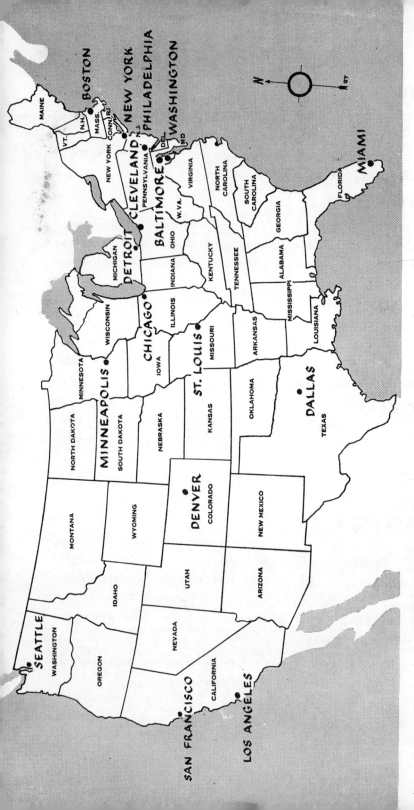

THE UNITED STATES OF AMERICA

LESSON ONE

1A   The plural forms of nouns

one book	one dress	one family
two books	two dresses	two families

coat	coats	church	churches	baby	babies
word	words	class	classes	story	stories
page	pages	dish	dishes	body	bodies
boy	boys	box	boxes	lady	ladies

1B   The plural forms of irregular nouns

man	men	child	children
woman	women	foot	feet

singular

plural

1C   The definite and indefinite articles

SPECIFIC   (the definite article)

singular:	the girl	the apple	the man
plural:	the girls	the apples	the men

GENERAL   (the indefinite article)

singular:	a girl	an apple	a man
plural:	girls	apples	men

1D   Adjectives with nouns

the book	the girl	an apple
the red book	the pretty girl	a delicious apple
the red books	the pretty girls	delicious apples

a good radio	a good car	a nice pie	a nice apple
a car radio	a radio car	an apple pie	a pie apple

1

1E The subject pronouns

		singular	plural
1	FIRST PERSON	I	we
2	SECOND PERSON	you	you
3	THIRD PERSON	he she it	they

1F The verb *be*

1	I am OR I'm	we are OR we're
2	you are OR you're	you are OR you're
3	he is OR he's she is OR she's it is OR it's	they are OR they're

E x a m p l e s :

I am sick.
He is happy.
She is here.
We are ready.
They are busy now.
It is in the room.
The boy is a student.

John is happy
The boy is happy.
The girl is happy.
The house is big.
The houses are big.
John and Frank are big.
The boys are students.

1G Statements, questions, and negatives

Statement:		The boy	is		very sick.
Question:	Is	the boy			very sick?
Negative:		The boy	is	not	very sick.

1H Contractions with *be*

-----	we aren't	OR	I'm not	we're not
you aren't	you aren't		you're not	you're not
he isn't	they aren't		he's not	they're not
she isn't			she's not	
it isn't			it's not	

2

EXERCISES FOR LESSON ONE

Exercise 1   Write the plural form.

1 girl _girls_   6 baby _BABIES._   11 class _CLASSES._

2 book _books_   7 man _MEN._   12 room _ROOMS._

3 dress _DRESSES._   8 box _BOXES._   13 woman _WOMEN._

4 boy _BOYS._   9 child _CHILDREN_   14 student _STUDENTS._

5 coat _COATS._   10 story _STORIES._   15 family _FAMILIES._

Exercise 2   Write _a_ or _an_ before each word

1 _a_ lady   6 _a_ child   11 _a_ book

2 _a_ dish   7 _an_ egg   12 _a_ family

3 _a_ word   8 _a_ student   13 _an_ apartment

4 _an_ apple   9 _a_ dress   14 _a_ man

5 _a_ coat   10 _a_ house   15 _an_ address

Exercise 3   Write the plural form.

1 the book _the books_   7 a baby _BABIES._

2 a box _boxes_   8 the woman _THE WOMEN._

3 the story _THE STORIES._   9 an apple _APPLES._

4 the room _THE ROOMS._   10 the child _THE CHILDREN._

5 a student _STUDENTS._   11 an address _ADDRESSES._

6 the boy _THE BOYS._   12 the page _THE PAGES._

3

Exercise 4 Write the plural form.

1 the red book _____ *the red books*

2 a white egg _____ *white eggs*

3 the tall boy _THE TALL BOYS._

4 a happy girl _HAPPY GIRLS._

5 an interesting story _INTERESTING STORIES._

6 a good radio _GOOD RADIOS._

7 the red car _THE RED CARS._

8 a tall man _TALL MEN._

9 the small child _THE SMALL CHILDREN._

10 the white house _THE WITHE HOUSES._

11 a pretty coat _PRETTY COASTS._

12 an orange dress _ORANGE DRESSES._

13 a difficult word _DIFFICULT WORDS._

14 a big family _BIG FAMILIES._

15 a new dress _NEW DRESSES._

16 the big car _THE BIG CARS._

17 the big house _THE BIG HOUSES._

18 a pretty dress _PRETTY DRESSES_

19 the tall girl _THE TALL GIRLS._

20 a good story _GOOD STORIES._

4

Exercise 5 Use _am_, _is_, or _are_.

1 She __is__ a girl.   _She is a girl._

2 I __AM__ a student.   _I AM A STUDENT._

3 They __ARE__ here now.   _THEY ARE HERE NOW_

4 It __is__ very pretty.   _IT is VERY PRETTY_

5 John __is__ an American.   _John is AN AMERICAN_

6 The sun __is__ very hot.   _THE SUN is VERY hOT._

7 I __AM__ happy today.   _I AM happy TODAY._

8 She __is__ from Japan.   _SHE is FROM JAPAN._

9 Mary __is__ pretty.   _MARY is PRETTY._

10 The boy __is__ a student.   _THE BOY is A STUDENT._

11 The apartment __is__ very big.   _THE APARTMENT is VERY BIG._

12 The two rooms __ARE__ very big.   _THE ROOMS ARE VERY BIG._

13 Mary and Helen __ARE__ students.   _MARY AN HELEN AIRE STUDENTS._

14 The big boxes __ARE__ heavy.   _THE BIG BOXES ARE HEAVY._

15 The girl __is__ in the room now.   _THE GIRL IS IN THE ROOM NOW._

16 The weather __is__ very nice today.   _THE WEATHER is VERY NICE TODAY_

17 The men __ARE__ from South America. _THE MEN ARE FROM SOUTH AMERICA_

18 John and Frank __ARE__ from Europe. _JOHN AND FRANK ARE FROM EUROPE_

19 You __ARE__ in the United States now. _YOU ARE IN THE UNITED STATES NOW_

20 The United States __is__ very big.   _THE UNITED STATES is VERY BIG_

5

Exercise 6 Change the underlined words to the plural.

1. <u>He is</u> here.   _They are here._

2. The <u>boy is a student</u>.   _The boys are students._

3. <u>She is</u> from Europe.   _____

4. <u>It is</u> pretty.   _____

5. <u>I am</u> ready now.   _____

6. <u>You are a student</u>.   _____

7. The <u>girl is</u> in the house.   _____

8. The <u>house is</u> very big.   _____

9. The <u>book is</u> interesting.   _____

10. <u>I am</u> sick today.   _____

11. The <u>man is a doctor</u>.   _____

12. The <u>woman is</u> from Japan.   _____

13. The <u>girl is a student</u>.   _____

14. <u>It is</u> very difficult.   _____

15. <u>He is an American</u>.   _____

16. The <u>car is</u> very big.   _____

17. The tall <u>boy is</u> nice.   _____

18. The new <u>radio is</u> here.   _____

19. The American <u>girl is</u> there.   _____

20. The tall <u>boy is a student</u>.   _____

Exercise 7   Make questions.

1   He is happy. _____ *Is he happy?*
2   She is pretty. _____
3   You are from Europe. _____
4   Mary is very happy. _____
5   They are ready now. _____
6   The boy is small. _____
7   The house is big. _____
8   They are students here. _____
9   Mr. Brown is busy now. _____
10 Mr. and Mrs. Smith are here. _____
11 English is very easy. _____
12 English is an easy language. _____
13 Mary and Helen are students. _____
14 The English book is interesting. _____
15 The children are in the house. _____

Exercise 8   Make negatives.

1   She is ready. _____ *She is not ready.*
2   English is easy. _____
3   They are tired. _____
4   Mr. Smith is here. _____
5   You are a teacher. _____
6   I am ready. _____
7   The book is heavy. _____
8   Mr. Brown is busy today. _____
9   The doctor is from Europe. _____
10 The tall boy is a good student. _____

7

Exercise 9 Make contractions with the underlined words.

1 She is very pretty. _____ *She's very pretty.*

2 He is not a doctor. _____

3 I am a student here. _____

4 We are from South America. _____

5 It is very cold today. _____

6 They are students here. _____

7 You are not a teacher. _____

8 I am not a doctor. _____

9 They are not ready yet. _____

10 They are not in the room. _____

11 It is very pretty. _____

12 It is not in the house. _____

13 It is not in the room. _____

14 I am not a student. _____

15 He is very handsome. _____

16 We are not ready yet. _____

17 She is not here now. _____

18 It is quite hot today. _____

19 It is not cold today. _____

20 I am not very tired. _____

21 You are a teacher. _____

22 He is not a teacher. _____

23 She is not a student. _____

24 It is interesting. _____

25 He is not very tall. _____

26 They are here now. _____

8

Pages 1 - 8

a 1	foot 1	page 1
address 3	Frank 2	pretty 1
am 2	from 5	quite 8
American 5	girl 1	radio 1
an 1	good 1	ready 2
and 2	handsome 8	red 1
apartment 3	happy 2	room 2
apple 1	he 2	she 2
are 2	heavy 5	she's 2
aren't 2	Helen 7	sick 2
baby 1	here 2	small 4
big 2	he's 2	Smith 7
body 1	hot 5	South America 4
book 1	house 2	story 1
box 1	I 2	student 2
boy 1	I'm 2	sun 5
Brown 7	in 2	tall 4
busy 2	interesting 4	teacher 7
car 1	is 2	the 1
child 1	isn't 2	they 2
children 1	it 2	they're 2
church 1	it's 2	tired 7
class 1	Japan 5	today 5
coat 1	John 2	two 1
cold 8	lady 1	the United States 5
delicious 1	language 7	very 5
difficult 4	man 1	we 2
dish 1	Mary 5	weather 5
doctor 6	men 1	we're 2
dress 1	Mr. 7	white 4
easy 7	Mrs. 7	woman 1
egg 3	new 4	women 1
English 7	nice 5	word 1
Europe 5	now 2	yet 8
family 1	one 1	you 2
feet 1	orange 4	you're 2

English is easy.

LESSON TWO

2A The simple present tense

The simple present tense describes a customary or repeated action. It also describes a general truth.

1	first person	I work	we work
2	second person	you work	you work
3	third person	he she works it	they work

Notice the spelling:

I work	I teach	I study
he works	she teaches	he studies

learn	learns	wash	washes	reply	replies
need	needs	miss	misses	cry	cries
write	writes	fix	fixes	try	tries
buy	buys	go	goes	fly	flies

E x a m p l e s :

I work every day.
I work in a store.
I work hard.
He studies English every day.
He studies very hard.
We always learn new words.
We always write the words.

The boy knows the answer.
The boy knows the man.
The man knows the boy.
The boy likes the girl.
The boys like the girl.
The girl likes the boy.
The girl likes the boys.

2B The simple present tense of *do* and *have*

1	I do	we do
2	you do	you do
3	he she does it	they do

1	I have	we have
2	you have	you have
3	he she has it	they have

2C Statements, questions, and negatives

Statement:		They			work	every day.
Question:	Do	they			work	every day?
Negative:		They	do	not	work	every day.

Statement:		He			studies	every day.
Question:	Does	he			study	every day?
Negative:		He	does	not	study	every day.

Statement:		Tom			has	a book.
Question:	Does	Tom			have	a book?
Negative:		Tom	does	not	have	a book.

2D The words *this* and *these*, *that* and *those*

NEAR THE SPEAKER

this boy	this girl	this apple	this red book
these boys	these girls	these apples	these red books

NOT NEAR THE SPEAKER

that boy	that girl	that apple	that red book
those boys	those girls	those apples	those red books

Examples:

This, that, these, those

This is a book.
This book is interesting.
These are cigarettes.
These cigarettes are white.
Is this a box?
Yes, that is a box.
Are these books interesting?
Those books aren't interesting.

That is a flower.
That flower is pretty.
Are those flowers yellow?
No, they're green.
Is that an ashtray?
Yes, it's an ashtray.
Are those flowers?
Yes, they're flowers.

2E Contractions with *do* and *that*

do not	=	don't
does not	=	doesn't

that is	=	that's

2F The words *in* and *on*

The table is ⌈in the room.⌉

The book is ⌈on the table.⌉

The book ⌈on the table⌉ is interesting.

The book ⌈on the table⌉ ⌈in the room⌉ is interesting.

IN The pencils are in the drawer.
   The flowers in the garden are white.
   John lives in the United States.
   He lives in New York.
   He works in a big store.

in?
on?

ON The picture is on the wall.
   The picture on the wall is pretty.
   The rug is on the floor.

2G Word Study

These words are singular: <u>money</u>, <u>news</u>, <u>family</u>, <u>the United States</u>.

   The money is on the table.
   The news is good today.
   That family is very big.
   The United States is very big.

This word is plural: <u>people</u>.

   Those people are from South America.

The word <u>handsome</u> usually describes males.
The word <u>good-looking</u> describes males or females.
The words <u>pretty</u> and <u>beautiful</u> describe females, children, and objects.

a handsome man	a pretty chair
a good-looking man	a beautiful child
a good-looking girl.	a beautiful woman
a pretty girl	a beautiful flower

12

Exercise 10 Use this or these.

1	_this_ picture	11	_____ books
2	_this_ page	12	_____ dish
3	_these_ words	13	_____ women
4	_____ flower	14	_____ child
5	_____ people	15	_____ weather
6	_____ classes	16	_____ news
7	_____ store	17	_____ coats
8	_____ erasers	18	_____ money
9	_____ car	19	_____ boxes
10	_____ church	20	_____ people

Exercise 11 Use that or those.

1	_that_ boy	11	_____ word
2	_those_ doctors	12	_____ children
3	_____ girls	13	_____ man
4	_____ women	14	_____ baby
5	_____ box	15	_____ books
6	_____ language	16	_____ ladies
7	_____ radio	17	_____ dress
8	_____ people	18	_____ news
9	_____ money	19	_____ books
10	_____ students	20	_____ woman

Exercise 12 Change these words to the plural form.

1	this book _these books_	11	that child _____
2	that table _those tables_	12	this class _____
3	this pencil _____	13	this word _____
4	that school _____	14	that store _____
5	this page _____	15	that dress _____
6	this car _____	16	this lesson _____
7	that man _____	17	that student _____
8	this house _____	18	that man _____
9	that picture _____	19	this country _____
10	that woman _____	20	that question _____

Exercise 13 Use <u>that</u> or <u>those</u>.

1 *That* picture is very interesting.   *That*
2 Is ——book interesting?   _____
3 ——tables are very big.   _____
4 Are ——men from Europe?   _____
5 Does ——woman like coffee?   _____
6 ——student has an automobile.   _____
7 ——children are very happy.   _____
8 ——windows are very big.   _____
9 Are ——boxes very heavy?   _____
10 Do ——girls come from Spain?   _____
11 ——tall girl is very pretty.   _____
12 ——questions are difficult.   _____
13 Is ——new student from China?   _____
14 Do —— men speak English?   _____
15 ——flowers are very beautiful.   _____
16 Does ——boy know——girls?   _____
17 Do you study——book every day?   _____
18 ——women are students here.   _____
19 —— boy is very smart.   _____
20 Do ——girls know the answer?   _____

Exercise 14

QUESTION	ANSWER
(Use <u>this</u> or <u>these</u>)	(Use <u>is</u> or <u>are</u>)

1 Is *this* a desk?   Yes, it *is* a desk.
2 Are —— pictures?   Yes, they —— pictures.
3 Is —— a cigarette?   No, that—— a cigar.
4 Is —— a coat?   No, it —— a suit.
5 Are —— photographs?   Yes, they —— photographs.
6 Is —— a penny?   Yes, that —— a penny.
7 Are —— nickels?   Yes, those —— nickels.
8 Is —— a shirt   No, it —— a blouse.
9 Is —— a blouse?   No, it —— a shirt.
10 Are —— dimes?   Yes, they —— dimes.
11 Are —— windows?   Yes, those —— windows.
12 Is —— a chair?   No, that —— a table.

14

Exercise 15   Use <u>have</u> or <u>has</u>.

1	He _has_ new shoes.	13	John and Mary——a car.
2	They _HAVE_ two books.	14	He and I——many friends.
3	John _has_ a pen.	15	The men——many books.
4	I _HAVE_ a new dress.	16	The children——toys.
5	She _HAS_ a red pencil.	17	The boy——a new suit.
6	We _HAVE_ a good teacher.	18	The women——new hats.
7	You _H_ a nice house.	19	The girl——a friend.
8	I —— an eraser.	20	Mr. Brown——a big house.
9	Mary——a red hat.	21	We —— three books.
10	Mr. Smith —— a car.	22	The man —— a big box.
11	I—— many friends.	23	The girl——a red suit.
12	We ——a small car.	24	She ——a pretty hat.

Exercise 16   Use <u>is</u> or <u>are</u>.

1   The children _are_ in the house.   _are_
2   The news ——very bad today.
3   The people —— here now.
4   The men —— good-looking.
5   The woman ——very pretty.
6   The family —— quite big.
7   The United States ——interesting.
8   The people ——from Europe.
9   The money _IS_ on the desk.
10 The girl _is_ very beautiful.

Exercise 17   Use <u>in</u> or <u>on</u>.

1   The students are _in_ the room now.   _in_
2   Does John work —— a store?
3   Is the photograph ——the front wall?
4   The book ——the table is interesting.
5   Is the rug——the floor pretty?
6   The two coats are —— the chair.
7   The flowers —— the garden are pretty.
8   Does Charles live —— South America?
9   The words ——this page are hard.
10 The words ——that book are difficult.

15

Exercise 18 Add words like <u>tall</u>, <u>new</u>, <u>pretty</u>, etc. Use fifteen different words.

1 a ——— boy   *a tall boy*
2 the —— girl
3 that —— book
4 an ——— car
5 the —— houses
6 those — students
7 the —— box
8 a ——— hat
9 an —— book
10 these — flowers
11 a ——— man
12 those — women
13 the —— words
14 a ——— lesson
15 the —— coat

Exercise 19 Use <u>do</u>, <u>does</u>, <u>am</u>, <u>are</u>, or <u>is</u>.

1 ___Do___ you know this word?   Do
2 ___Is___ that boy from England?   Is
3 ——— the men come from Europe?
4 ——— those students study hard?
5 ——— the people in the room?
6 ——— the books on the table?
7 ——— the money on the table?
8 ——— Charles like coffee?
9 ——— you from South America?
10 ——— the words seem hard?
11 ——— Charles and John work hard?
12 ——— the women students here?
13 ——— she like milk in the coffee?
14 ——— Miss Brown from the United States?
15 ——— Mr. and Mrs. Smith teach English?
16 ——— the news good today?
17 ——— the man study in this class?
18 ——— that an ashtray on the table?
19 ——— you know the new student?
20 ——— they in the room now?

Does this seem hard?

16

Exercise 20 Make contractions with the underlined words.

1 I <u>do not</u> like coffee. _____ *I don't like coffee.*
2 He <u>does not</u> know the girl. _____
3 They <u>do not</u> study hard. _____
4 She <u>does not</u> smoke cigarettes. _____
5 We <u>do not</u> spend much money. _____
6 He <u>is</u> very handsome. _____
7 <u>I am</u> a doctor. _____
8 <u>You are</u> a good student. _____
9 He <u>does not</u> have a pencil. _____
10 <u>It is</u> very hot today. _____
11 He <u>is not</u> tired now. _____
12 We <u>do not</u> work every day. _____
13 They <u>are not</u> here now. _____
14 <u>I am</u> not a doctor. _____
15 I <u>do not</u> like coffee very much. _____

Exercise 21 Use <u>doesn't</u>, <u>don't</u>, <u>aren't</u>, <u>isn't</u> or <u>am not</u>.

1 The book _isn't_ on the table.   *isn't*
2 Those students _____ study very hard.   _____
3 The men _____ from South America.   _____
4 I _____ ready yet.   _____
5 That woman _____ come from Europe.   _____
6 The children _____ in the room.   _____
7 Those people _____ like coffee.   _____
8 Miss Smith _____ a student here.   _____
9 Mr. and Mrs. Brown _____ study English.   _____
10 The money _____ on the table now.   _____
11 That student _____ know the answer.   _____
12 You _____ from England.   _____
13 We _____ know that word.   _____
14 Mr. Brown _____ busy today.   _____
15 Charles _____ work in that store.   _____
16 The girls _____ in the front room.   _____
17 She _____ have a new car.   _____
18 They _____ spend very much money.   _____
19 The words on that page _____ difficult.   _____
20 We _____ have many friends yet.   _____

17

Exercise 22 Change <u>I</u> to <u>he</u> or <u>she</u>.

1 I know the answer. _____ *He knows the answer.*
2 I'm not ready yet. _____
3 I like candy very much. _____
4 I'm very tired now. _____
5 I don't know that boy. _____
6 I'm quite hungry now. _____
7 I have a new suit. _____
8 I don't have a car. _____
9 I work in a big store. _____
10 I have many friends. _____
11 I don't have the money. _____
12 I learn new words every day. _____
13 I'm a student in that class. _____
14 I don't like coffee very much. _____
15 I write letters every day. _____

Exercise 23 Change <u>he</u>, <u>she</u>, and <u>it</u> to <u>they</u>.

1 He studies very hard. _____ *They study very hard.*
2 It's very pretty. _____
3 He knows English very well. _____
4 She doesn't know that man. _____
5 He speaks French very well. _____
6 She's not very old. _____
7 He goes to school every day. _____
8 She lives in the United States. _____
9 He has a new car. _____
10 She's ready now. _____
11 He doesn't buy cigarettes every day. ___
12 She doesn't have the book. _____
13 It's in the front room now. _____
14 She works in a big store. _____
15 It's quite difficult. _____
16 He doesn't know the answer. _____
17 She has many friends. _____
18 He lives in an apartment. _____
19 She doesn't have a big house. _____
20 It's quite big. _____

Exercise 24 Change the underlined words to the plural.

(part one)

1 It is beautiful. _____ *They are beautiful.*
2 The boy isn't a student. _____
3 That man doesn't speak French. _____
4 The child isn't in the room. _____
5 This house is very old. _____
6 That boy isn't a student. _____
7 Does this book seem hard? _____
8 That woman is a doctor. _____
9 This word is quite difficult. _____
10 Is the teacher from the United States? _____
11 Does he have a new car? _____
12 I don't like coffee. _____
13 This word isn't new. _____
14 That new car is beautiful. _____
15 Are you a student here? _____

(part two)

16 He has a new suit. _____
17 He has a big house. _____
18 That tall man is a doctor. _____
19 This is an easy lesson. _____
20 Is the house very big? _____
21 Does she work in a store? _____
22 The flower is very beautiful. _____
23 The new student isn't here yet. _____
24 This car isn't very big. _____
25 Are you a doctor? _____
26 Does he live in New York? _____
27 She lives in the United States. _____
28 This house is quite big. _____
29 That pretty girl is from Japan. _____
30 The student in that class is from Italy. _____
31 This lesson is very easy. _____
32 Is that woman from Europe? _____
33 That new word is difficult. _____

Exercise 25 Change these statements to questions.

(part one)

1 They like coffee. _____ *Do they like coffee?*
2 The boy knows the answer. _____
3 The boys work in a store. _____
4 You know many new words. _____
5 John studies very hard. _____
6 They go to school every day. _____
7 She asks many questions. _____
8 They spend much money. _____
9 Mr. Brown speaks very fast. _____
10 You understand the lesson. _____
11 They write many letters. _____
12 He knows many English words. _____
13 Mary speaks Spanish well. _____
14 The boys like coffee. _____
15 The women come from Europe. _____

(part two)

16 Mr. Brown teaches English. _____
17 The new student is smart. _____
18 Helen lives in New York. _____
19 English is an easy language. _____
20 The men speak French. _____
21 That's a new rug. _____
22 Those people like this country. _____
23 That tall boy is an American. _____
24 Mary and Helen are students here. _____
25 That student studies every day. _____
26 The English book is interesting. _____
27 The baby cries very much. _____
28 The pretty girl is from Brazil. _____
29 This seems very difficult. _____
30 He writes letters every day. _____
31 Charles speaks Portuguese. _____
32 They go there every year. _____
33 It's an interesting story. _____

Exercise 26 Change these statements to negatives.

(part one)

1 I know that word. _____ *I don't know that word.*
2 He understands that lesson. _____
3 They go to school every day. _____
4 She asks many questions. _____
5 Frank writes many letters. _____
6 The men come from Brazil. _____
7 The tall woman speaks very fast. _____
8 That boy works very hard. _____
9 I study the lesson every day. _____
10 Those people like coffee. _____
11 I speak French well. _____
12 Those boys live in Chicago. _____
13 Mr. Smith teaches English. _____
14 We know many English words. _____
15 John and Frank have many friends. _____

(part two)

16 They spend much money. _____
17 The box is very heavy. _____
18 She studies every afternoon. _____
19 The tall student is from Spain. _____
20 He speaks that language. _____
21 That's an old church. _____
22 Mr. Brown works very hard. _____
23 The girls are in the front room. _____
24 The new students understand this. _____
25 That woman is an American. _____
26 Mr. Brown flies to England every year. _____
27 The English book is on the table. _____
28 I work in a big store. _____
29 The red pencils are in the drawer. _____
30 We need money. _____
31 Mary has a new dress. _____
32 They're from South America. _____
33 She likes that class very much. _____

21

VOCABULARY FOR LESSON TWO

Pages 10 - 21

afternoon 21
answer 10
ashtray 11
ask 20
automobile 14
bad 15
beautiful 12
blouse 14
Brazil 20
buy 10
candy 18
chair 12
Charles 15
Chicago 21
China 14
cigar 14
cigarette 11
coffee 16
come 14
country 12
cry 10
day 10
desk 15
dime 14
do 10
does 10
doesn't 12
don't 12
drawer 12
England 16
eraser 15
every 10
fast 20
fix 10
floor 14
flower 11
fly 10

French 18
friend 15
front 18
garden 12
go 10
good-looking 12
green 11
hard 10
has 10
hat 15
have 10
hungry 18
Italy 19
know 10
learn 10
lesson 19
letter 16
live 12
many 15
milk 16
Miss 16
miss 10
money 12
much 18
need 10
news 12
New York 12
nickel 14
old 18
on 12
pen 15
pencil 15
penny 14
people 12
photograph 14
picture 12
Portuguese 20

question 13
reply 10
rug 14
seem 16
shirt 14
shoes 15
smart 14
Spain 14
Spanish 20
speak 18
spend 17
store 10
study 10
suit 15
table 12
teach 10
that 11
that's 12
these 11
this 11
those 11
three 15
toy 15
try 10
understand 21
wall 12
wash 10
well 18
window 14
work 10
write 10
yellow 11
year 20

English is easy.

22

LESSON THREE

3A The continuous present tense

1	I am working	we are working
2	you are working	you are working
3	he she is working it	they are working

The continuous present tense expresses the action of the present moment. It also expresses a temporary action with definite time limits.

PRESENT MOMENT: I am writing a letter right now. He is waiting for you. They are talking to Professor Taylor.

TEMPORARY ACTION: I am studying English at N. Y. U. this semester. That man is writing a book about Lincoln.

Important exception:

These verbs usually occur in the simple present tense: believe, belong, contain, cost, desire, dislike, feel (for opinion), forget, forgive, happen, hate, have (for possession), hear, know, like, love, mean, need, notice, occur, owe, own, prefer, possess, recognize, refuse, remember, see, seem, smell, suppose, taste, think (for opinion), understand, want.

SPELLING THE "-ING" FORM (the present participle):

work	write	run
working	writing	running

visit	visiting	come	coming	begin	beginning
study	studying	live	living	stop	stopping
go	going	give	giving	shut	shutting

23

3B Statements, questions, and negatives

Statement:		Mr. Brown	is		eating	now.
Question:	Is	Mr. Brown			eating	now?
Negative:		Mr. Brown	is	not	eating	now.

3C The two present tenses

Compare these examples:

I study every day.   I go to class two times a week.
I am studying now.   I am going to class right now.

Mr. Brown usually eats breakfast at the cafeteria.
Mr. Brown is eating breakfast at the cafeteria now.

John and Frank work at that store every Saturday.
John and Frank are working at that store today.

BUT (hear, like, know, etc. - see page 23):

I hear a noise!   I see an airplane.
She knows the answer.   We understand it.
He wants some coffee.   They like milk very much.

3D Questions with the word *what*

Simple statement:			That	is	a book.
Simple question:		Is	that		a book?
Question with what:	What	is	that?		

Simple statement:			Those	are	books.
Simple question:		Are	those		books?
Question with what:	What	are	those?		

What is it?   What is this?   What are they?
It's a chair.   That's an egg.   They're chairs.

What is that?   What's that?   What are these?
It's an airplane.   It's a table.   Those are dishes.

Notice this contraction: | what is = what's |

24

3E The expressions *there is* and *there are*

Singular:	There	is	one student in the room.
Plural:	There	are	two students in the room.

Statements, questions, and negatives:

	There	are		many students in the room.
Are	there			many students in the room?
	There	are	not	many students in the room.

Notice the contraction:

there is	=	there's

3F The prepositions *to* and *from*

TO   We go to school every day.
They go to Mexico every year.
He sends many letters to Charles.
He is writing a letter to Charles now.
She is talking to Tom right now.
John is speaking to the teacher now.
The students are listening to the radio.

FROM   Charles is from Italy.
Charles comes from Italy.
The boy from Italy is quite short.
We receive a letter from John every week.

3G Idioms

go to bed: The children usually go to bed at nine o'clock.

in a hurry: John is always in a hurry. I'm in a hurry now.

in general: In general, the English lessons are quite easy.

on time: That doctor always comes to this class on time.

pay attention to: The students pay attention to the teacher.

right now: I am busy right now. She's working right now.

EXERCISES FOR LESSON THREE

Exercise 27   Use <u>this</u> or <u>these</u>.

1	_this_ question	11	_____ chairs
2	_these_ people	12	_____ books
3	_____ house	13	_____ tables
4	_____ hospital	14	_____ page
5	_____ flowers	15	_____ apple
6	_____ radio	16	_____ pen
7	_____ dresses	17	_____ notebook
8	_____ news	18	_____ words
9	_____ children	19	_____ exercises
10	_____ answer	20	_____ chapter

Exercise 28   If necessary, use <u>a</u> or <u>an</u>.

1	That's _a_ door.	11	I'm teacher.
2	That's _an_ orange.	12	They're students.
3	These are pencils.	13	That's camera.
4	That's umbrella.	14	This is picture.
5	He's lawyer.	15	Those are matches.
6	She's nurse.	16	The boy is student.
7	Those are apples.	17	It's notebook.
8	This is match.	18	That's radio.
9	Those are old books.	19	Those are dresses.
10	This is overcoat.	20	They're exercises.

Exercise 29   Make contractions with the underlined words.

1 <u>They are</u> in the room. _____ _They're in the room._
2 <u>I am</u> reading right now. _____
3 <u>He is</u> not ready yet. _____
4 <u>There is</u> a book on the table. _____
5 <u>What is</u> that? _____
6 We <u>are not</u> studying now. _____
7 He <u>does not</u> know Tom. _____
8 <u>There is</u> a box on the table. _____
9 We <u>do not</u> like coffee. _____
10 She <u>is not</u> listening to the radio. _____

Exercise 30 Use <u>there is</u> or <u>there are</u> and <u>in the room</u> with these words. Notice the examples.

1	a desk	_There is a desk in the room._
2	tables	_There are tables in the room._

3	a picture	13	seven chairs
4	chairs	14	many students
5	a telephone	15	a big window
6	flowers	16	several boys
7	people	17	some men
8	a blackboard	18	a large door
9	photographs	19	many people
10	a window	20	only two chairs
11	three maps	21	a long table
12	a wastebasket	22	several young girls.

Exercise 31 Complete these sentences.

QUESTION

1 What _is_ that?
2 What — this?
3 What — those?
4 What — these?
5 What — this?
6 What — that?
7 What — those?
8 What — ——?
9 What — ——?
10 What — ——?
11 What — ——?
12 What — ——?
13 What — ——?
14 What — ——?
15 What — ——?
16 What — ——?
17 What — ——?
18 What — ——?
19 What — ——?
20 What — ——?

ANSWER

That _is_ _a_ book.
That —— ——pencil.
They —— shoes.
Those —— cigars.
It —— — window.
This —— — camera.
They —— photographs.
It —— — film.
—— —— — bus.
—— —— — pennies.
—— —— — nickel.
—— —— dimes.
—— —— — dollar.
—— —— — shirt.
—— —— blouses.
—— —— matches.
—— —— — apple.
—— —— chairs.
—— —— — umbrella.
—— —— maps.

27

Exercise 32 Write the -ing form of each verb.

1	work _____working_____	11	fix _____
2	study _____studying_____	12	shine _____
3	hold _____	13	answer _____
4	read _____	14	cry _____
5	shut _____	15	go _____
6	come _____	16	live _____
7	watch _____	17	put _____
8	pronounce _____	18	give _____
9	play _____	19	rain _____
10	write _____	20	begin _____

Exercise 33 Use in, on, to, or from.

1 Do they receive a letter—— John every week? _from_
2 Does Charles come—— South America? _____
3 Is the student writing —— the blackboard? _____
4 Is Tom speaking—— Charles now? _____
5 Are you writing a letter ——Frank? _____
6 Do you go——school every day? _____
7 Are there pretty flowers —— the garden? _____
8 Is there a picture —— the wall? _____
9 Is she listening—— the radio now? _____
10 Are the boys —— a hurry? _____
11 Do you go —— bed late every night? _____
12 Does Tom come —— time every day? _____
13 Are they paying attention —— the teacher? _____
14 Do they like this country ——general? _____
15 Is he studying——the library now? _____
16 Do you receive letters —— them every week? _____
17 Is he talking——the new student? _____
18 Do you come ——Brazil? _____
19 Are they listening —— the news now? _____
20 Are you writing —— that notebook? _____
21 Are you writing —— that page? _____
22 Do the children always go —— bed early? _____
23 Are you putting the flowers ——the table? _____
24 Do you send many letters ——those boys? _____
25 Does she always study——that room? _____

28

Exercise 34 Change the underlined words to the plural.

1 The box is very big. _____ *The boxes are very big.*
2 That man isn't a doctor. _____
3 The student is listening to the radio. _____
4 That tall boy comes from Sweden. _____
5 Does he have a car? _____
6 She has a new dress. _____
7 The child is sleeping right now. _____
8 Are you a teacher? _____
9 This English class is interesting. _____
10 That woman is spelling the words. _____
11 It is a big house. _____
12 The girl is talking to Mr. Brown. _____
13 What is that? _____
14 That man is from Germany. _____
15 There is a book on the table. _____
16 He knows that word. _____
17 The teacher is pronouncing the words. _____
18 There is a chair in that room. _____
19 This red dress is very pretty. _____
20 He has a new overcoat. _____

Exercise 35 Use am, is, or are.

1 The boys *are* studying right now.   *are*
2 Helen and Mary —— reading the lesson.   _____
3 I —— listening to the radio right now.   _____
4 She —— beginning the lesson now.   _____
5 The baby —— crying now.   _____
6 The men —— fixing the car.   _____
7 The sun —— shining today.   _____
8 Mr. Smith —— writing a book.   _____
9 The people —— sitting in that room.   _____
10 —— you learning those new words?   _____
11 —— those boys talking to John?   _____
12 —— he working right now?   _____
13 —— the women studying the lesson?   _____
14 —— it raining very hard?   _____
15 —— the children playing right now?   _____

29

Exercise 36 Use the continuous present tense of each verb.

1 He (open) the door now. *He is opening the door now.*
2 John (study) the lesson now. _____
3 The girls (shop) at the store. _____
4 The children (play) in the yard. _____
5 The men (drop) the boxes on the floor. _____
6 The instructor (give) the book to John. _____
7 The boys (come) into the house now. _____
8 The women (talk) to the teacher now. _____
9 Mr. Smith (look) at the newspaper now. _____
10 The professor (begin) the lesson now. _____
11 The clerk (count) the money carefully. _____
12 They (study) the new words now. _____
13 The boy (hit) the ball now. _____
14 He (run) into the building. _____
15 She (repeat) the words carefully. _____
16 Frank and John (smile) at the pretty girl. _____
17 John and I (carry) the chairs into the room. _____
18 The children (look) at the pictures. _____
19 The students (shut) the windows in the room. _____
20 The doctor (write) the new word. _____

Exercise 37 Use <u>am not</u>, <u>isn't</u>, <u>aren't</u>, <u>don't</u>, or <u>doesn't</u>.

1 The book *isn't* on the table.   _____*isn't*_____
2 I —— listening to the radio now.   _____
3 I —— listen to the radio every day.   _____
4 There —— a table in that room.   _____
5 It —— rain here every week.   _____
6 It —— raining outside now.   _____
7 They —— study every afternoon.   _____
8 The boys —— studying the lesson now.   _____
9 She —— know that word.   _____
10 Mr. and Mrs. Williams —— eating now.   _____
11 They —— eat here every day.   _____
12 We —— go to the library every day.   _____
13 John and I —— ready yet.   _____
14 The people —— like coffee very much.   _____
15 The children —— playing now.   _____

30

Exercise 38   Change these statements to questions.

(part one)

1   It is raining now. _____   *Is it raining now?*
2   He is studying English. _____
3   There is a picture on the wall. _____
4   She is opening the door now. _____
5   They are watching the game. _____
6   There are many chairs in that room. _____
7   The women are waiting now. _____
8   There is a big table in that room. _____
9   Mr. Williams is beginning the class now. _____
10 The boys are eating right now. _____
11 The man is reading the book. _____
12 There are many people in this class. _____
13 The sun is shining today. _____
14 They are coming into the room now. _____
15 Those dresses are very cheap. _____

(part two)

16 John is opening the window now. _____
17 There are more chairs in the other room. _____
18 The movie is starting right now. _____
19 They are working very hard. _____
20 The children are in the front room. _____
21 Mr. Williams is teaching now. _____
22 The short boy is from Brazil. _____
23 The boy from Brazil is in this class. _____
24 There are enough towels in the bathroom. _____
25 They are ready now. _____
26 The girls are studying the lesson. _____
27 The boys are fixing the old car. _____
28 You are watching television now. _____
29 The children are listening to the radio. _____
30 Mary is listening to the music. _____
31 These shoes are expensive. _____
32 He is reading the newspaper now. _____
33 There is a mistake on this page. _____
34 They are pronouncing the new words. _____

Exercise 39 Change these statements to negatives.

(part one)

1 He is reading now. _____ *He isn't reading now.*
2 They are working hard now. _____
3 You are studying English now. _____
4 It is raining right now. _____
5 The men are coming into the room. _____
6 The sun is shining now. _____
7 She is shutting the window. _____
8 It is snowing outside now. _____
9 He is holding the package now. _____
10 The children are sleeping now. _____
11 They are sitting in the room. _____
12 John and Tom are studying the lesson. _____
13 The girls are writing on the blackboard. _____
14 There is a picture on the wall. _____
15 The tall boy is from Europe. _____

(part two)

16 I am watching the game now. _____
17 Mr. Williams is reading the newspaper. _____
18 The students are listening to the teacher. _____
19 John is walking with the Italian student. _____
20 They are pronouncing the new words now. _____
21 There are many people in the room. _____
22 She is looking at the pictures now. _____
23 Mary and Helen are studying in the library. _____
24 The chairs are in the front room. _____
25 The woman is talking to the teacher. _____
26 The children are playing in the yard. _____
27 There are many chairs in the other room. _____
28 Tom is looking at the magazine now. _____
29 The student is opening the door now. _____
30 The students are asking questions now. _____
31 I am smoking a cigarette now. _____
32 Charles is washing the car now. _____
33 Those houses are very large. _____
34 The boys are fixing the car now. _____

Pages 23 - 32

about 23
airplane 24
at 30
ball 30
bathroom 31
bedroom 31
begin 23
blackboard 32
breakfast 24
building 30
bus 27
camera 27
carefully 30
carry 30
chapter 26
cheap 31
clerk 30
count 30
door 31
exercise 26
expensive 31
film 27
game 31
Germany 29
give 23
hear 23
hit 30
hold 23
hospital 26
instructor 30
into 30
Italian 32
large 27
lawyer 26
library 28
Lincoln 23

listen 25
long 27
look 30
map 27
match 26
Mexico 25
more 31
movie 31
music 31
newspaper 30
noise 24
notebook 26
nurse 26
only 27
open 30
other 31
overcoat 26
package 32
play 30
pronounce 29
put 28
rain 28
read 31
receive 25
refuse 23
repeat 30
Saturday 24
school 25
see 23
semester 23
send 25
seven 27
several 27
shine 31
shop 30
shut 23

sit 29
sleep 29
smell 23
smile 30
snow 31
some 24
spell 29
start 31
stop 23
telephone 27
television 31
there's 25
think 23
Tom 25
towel 31
umbrella 26
visit 23
want 23
wastebasket 27
watch 31
week 25
what 24
what's 24
Williams 30
yard 30

English is an easy language.

33

LESSON FOUR

4A Summary of the present tenses

CONTINUOUS

He is working now.
Is he working now?
He isn't working now.

SIMPLE

He works every day.
Does he work every day?
He doesn't work every day.

The continuous present tense expresses the action of the present moment. It also expresses a temporary action with definite time limits.

The simple present tense expresses a customary or repeated action. It also expresses a general truth.

Examples:

I am studying right now.
He is writing a book.
It is snowing outside now.
Are you listening now?
It isn't raining now.

I study every afternoon.
He writes a page every day.
It often snows in the winter.
Do you listen all the time?
It doesn't rain every day.

Note:

Certain verbs (<u>hear</u>, <u>like</u>, <u>see</u>, etc. - see page 23) occur only in the simple present tense form.

4B Short Answers (I)

QUESTION

Is that man a doctor?

Is John studying English?

Does that girl like coffee?

Is there a chair in that room?

SHORT ANSWER

Yes, he is. No, he isn't.

Yes, he is. No, he isn't.

Yes, she does. No, she doesn't.

Yes, there is. No, there isn't.

4C The word *what* with the present tenses

Simple statement:			He	wants	a car.
Simple question:		Does	he	want	a car?
Question with what:	What	does	he	want?	

Simple statement:			He	is	holding	a box.
Simple question:		Is	he		holding	a box?
Question with what:	What	is	he		holding?	

General question:	What	is	he	doing?

Examples:

What is she wearing?	She's wearing a blue dress.
What are you doing?	I'm studying the lesson.
What do you see?	I see an airplane.
What does he want?	He wants some coffee.
What does he do?	He teaches English.

4D The imperative forms

Commands, orders, directions, and some requests take the imperative form. The word <u>you</u> does not usually occur. The singular and plural forms are the same.

Positive:	Open the door.	Study this page.
Negative:	Don't open the door.	Don't study that page.

Positive:	Go away!	Be careful!
Negative:	Don't go away!	Don't be late!

4E Polite forms

LOOK!

Imperative:			Open the door.	
Polite:		Please	open the door.	
Polite:			Open the door,	please.
Very polite:	Would you	please	open the door.	
Very polite:	Would you		open the door,	please.

35

Imperative:		Don't open the door.	
Polite request:	Please	don't open the door.	
		Don't open the door,	please.

4F Suggestions with *let's*

Let's introduces a suggestion. It includes the speaker.

Positive:	Let's		go to the store.
Negative:	Let's	not	go to the store.

Let's		eat.
Let's	not	eat.

The form let's don't also occurs. However, let's not is
probably more current. In addition, let's not is an easier
form for non-native speakers of English.

4G The preposition *at*

Mr. Smith is looking at the newspaper.
The girls are shopping at the grocery store.
Mary is laughing at the funny joke.
They are sitting at the table.
There is someone at the door now.

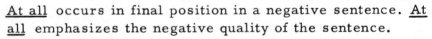

Notice these special uses:

John always studies at home.
The boys are at school now.

At all occurs in final position in a negative sentence. At
all emphasizes the negative quality of the sentence.

I don't have any money at all.
There aren't any chairs here at all.

4H Idioms

all right: That's all right. Close the door. -- All right.

at least: Write at least ten sentences with these new words.

at once: Close the door at once!   Do that work at once!

cash a check: Charles is cashing a check at the bank now.

first of all: Let's go to a movie. -- All right. But first
of all, let's eat.   Please finish that lesson first of all.

for example: Spanish words and English words are often similar.   For example, "cheque" is similar to "check."

for now: Let's do that work the other way just for now.

for sale: That pretty new house is for sale.   Let's buy it!

get ready: The girls are getting ready for the party now.

get sick: Mrs. Brown often gets sick on long trips by air.

get time off: Does Charles ever get time off from work?

get up: He wakes up at 7:00 a.m.   He gets up immediately.

go for a walk: It's too hot here.   Let's go for a short walk.

go over: Let's go over the last two lessons again, John.

go to bed: He usually goes to bed between eleven and twelve.

here and there: We find examples of that here and there.

look out: Look out!   A car is coming at you very fast!

now and then: They go to a baseball game now and then.

put away: Put away your coat.   Don't leave it on the chair.

right away: Please finish the two assignments right away.

sit down: Sit down here, please.   Don't sit down in that seat.

stand up: Don't stand up.   Sit down in a comfortable chair.

take a trip: Let's take a trip to South America next year.

take time out: Let's take some time out from this work!

turn off: One light is enough.   Please turn off the other one.

turn on: It's dark here.   Please turn on the floor lamp.

turn down: Mr. Brown often turns down offers like that.

37

EXERCISES FOR LESSON FOUR

Exercise 40

Use this or these.

1 _this_____ notebook
2 _these____ umbrellas
3 _____ exercise
4 _____ matches
5 _____ sugar
6 _____ packages
7 _____ towels
8 _____ newspaper
9 _____ game
10 _____ map

Exercise 41

Use that or those.

1 _that_____ bus
2 _____ news
3 _____ music
4 _____ libraries
5 _____ people
6 _____ wastebasket
7 _____ buildings
8 _____ yard
9 _____ games
10 _____ lawyers

Exercise 42   If necessary, add a or an.

1 That's _a_ pencil.
2 Those are   doors.
3 These are   oranges.
4 This is   toy.
5 They're   lawyers.
6 He's   doctor.
7 That's   apple.
8 These are   matches.
9 This is   old book.
10 Those are   overcoats.

11 I'm   student.
12 They're   teachers.
13 Those are   cameras.
14 That's   photograph.
15 This is   match.
16 Mary is   student.
17 The boys are   students.
18 This is   dress.
19 These are   exercises.
20 That's   notebook.

Exercise 43   Make contractions with the underlined words.

1 That is a book. *(That's)*
2 What is that?
3 That is a picture.
4 What is this?
5 That is a box.
6 There is a box here.
7 What is that?
8 That is a shoe.
9 What is this?
10 That is a mirror.

11 He is very strong.
12 I am not a student.
13 I do not like candy.
14 We are not tired.
15 She does not understand.
16 What is he making?
17 It is not difficult.
18 There is a man here.
19 They do not like that.
20 What is she doing?

Exercise 44 Use these verbs in orders and directions. Write the negative form also.

1	shut

Shut the door.
Don't shut the door.

2	learn	7	give	12	bring	
3	close	8	ask	13	pass	
4	write	9	answer	14	read	
5	go	10	open	15	practice	
6	come	11	study	16	pronounce	

Exercise 45 Use the sentences from exercise 44. Write these polite forms:

1 Shut the door.

Please shut the door.
Would you please shut the door.

Exercise 46 Use the sentences from exercise 44. Write the polite negative form.

1 Don't shut the door. _____ *Please don't shut the door.*

Exercise 47 Write suggestions with <u>let's</u>. Use these verbs.

1 read

Let's read the paper.

2	study	8	visit	14	wash	
3	go	9	call	15	spell	
4	buy	10	sit	16	watch	
5	listen	11	see	17	play	
6	finish	12	drink	18	try	
7	learn	13	speak	19	walk	

Exercise 48 Use the sentences from exercise 47. Write the negative forms of those suggestions.

1 Let's read the paper. _____ *Let's not read the paper.*

Exercise 49   Give short answers to these questions.

1 Does the man like coffee? Yes, *he does.*
2 Is Mrs. Smith here? No, *she isn't.*
3 Are you ready now? Yes, _____
4 Is there a book on the desk? Yes, _____
5 Does that student work hard? No, _____
6 Are the children sleeping now? Yes, _____
7 Does Tom study every night? No, _____
8 Do you like milk? Yes, _____
9 Is Mr. Smith a doctor? No, _____
10 Are you working right now? Yes, _____
11 Are there dishes on the table? No, _____
12 Do they like the United States? Yes, _____
13 Is this car very expensive? No, _____
14 Does he understand English? Yes, _____
15 Are there many people here? No, _____
16 Does Miss Brown feel well today? No, _____
17 Do dogs like bones? Yes, _____
18 Does a tree need water? Yes, _____
19 Is there a light in that room? No, _____
20 Do you know the answer? Yes, _____

Exercise 50   Select the correct verb for each sentence.

1 Is he (work, working) today?   *working*
2 Do you (know, knowing) the answer?   _____
3 She's (study, studying) the new words.   _____
4 Does he (like, liking) that class?   _____
5 She's (listen, listening) to the radio.   _____
6 Is Betty (put, putting) away the dishes?   _____
7 Does he (go, going) there now and then?   _____
8 Are they (take, taking) a course in English? _____
9 Do you (take, taking) many examinations?   _____
10 Is George (cash, cashing) a check now?   _____
11 I'm (write, writing) a letter to Mary.   _____
12 Do you (watch, watching) baseball games?   _____
13 Is she (finish, finishing) the work now?   _____
14 Do you always (learn, learning) the words?   _____
15 They're (read, reading) the paper now.   _____

Exercise 51 Write the correct words in the blank spaces.

	QUESTION with <u>what</u>	ANSWER
1	What is that?	That _is_ a pencil.
2	What are those?	Those —— notebooks.
3	What — he carrying?	He's —— a book.
4	What — you reading?	We're —— a magazine.
5	What — you want?	I want —— glass of water.
6	What — he need?	He needs —— pencil.
7	What — —— ?	Those —— flowers.
8	What — —— ?	That's — city park.
9	What — — wearing?	She's —— a suit.
10	What — — see?	I see a big building.
11	What — — holding?	They're —— a big box.
12	What — —— ?	That —— a camera.
13	What — — studying?	We're —— the new lesson.
14	What — —— ?	It's —— watch.
15	What — —— ?	They're socks.

what?

16	What _is that_ ?	That's a suitcase.
17	What ——————?	Those are shoes.
18	What ——————?	He wants some coffee.
19	What ——————?	They are moving the piano.
20	What ——————?	I am writing a letter.
21	What ——————?	She needs a new dress.
22	What ——————?	This is a radio.
23	What ——————?	We are making a dress.
24	What ——————?	These are photographs.
25	What ——————?	He wants a new suit.

26	_What are you studying?_	We're studying the new words.
27	——————?	I'm reading a magazine
28	——————?	It's a check.
29	——————?	He's writing some sentences.
30	——————?	She wants some tea.
31	——————?	That word means "young boy."
32	——————?	I'm reading right now.
33	——————?	He works in a store.
34	——————?	She's studying right now.
35	——————?	It means "very tall building."

41

Exercise 52 Use <u>in</u>, <u>on</u>, <u>at</u>, <u>to</u>, or <u>from</u>.

(part one)

1	The new student is _from_ Cuba.	_from_
2	The books are —— the shelf.	————
3	Tom lives —— San Francisco.	————
4	The students are —— the classroom.	————
5	The rug is —— the floor.	————
6	Ralph comes —— Europe.	————
7	We go —— concerts now and then.	————
8	Do you go —— bed late?	————
9	Does he come —— school —— time?	————
10	Please pay attention —— this.	————
11	—— general, I enjoy movies.	————
12	That student is always —— a hurry.	————
13	Let's listen —— the radio now!	————
14	They're looking —— the photographs.	————
15	I don't like coffee —— all.	————

(part two)

16	Is Elizabeth —— home now?	————
17	Listen! Someone is —— the door.	————
18	They're laughing —— the joke.	————
19	Finish that work —— once!	————
20	I don't have any paper —— all.	————
21	I know —— least two thousand words.	————
22	I usually go —— sleep right away.	————
23	We send a letter —— John once a week.	————
24	We receive letters —— John every week.	————
25	Is Charles talking —— the teacher?	————
26	The lawyer —— Colombia is here now.	————
27	The pictures are —— the side wall.	————
28	There are many trees —— the park.	————
29	The words —— this page are easy.	————
30	The words —— that book are hard.	————
31	—— general, I like this city very much.	————
32	The man is looking —— the magazine.	————
33	Is the man —— France —— this class?	————
34	Please sit down —— this comfortable chair.	————

Exercise 53 Change these statements into questions.

(part one)

1 They like coffee. _____ *Do they like coffee?*
2 He is studying English. _____ *Is he studying English?*
3 She speaks very fast. _____
4 It is raining now. _____
5 You are working hard. _____
6 John is reading now. _____
7 She dances very well. _____
8 The boy lives in Chicago. _____
9 They are eating now. _____
10 You study very hard. _____

(part two)

11 The movie is starting now. _____
12 Frank studies very hard every night. _____
13 They travel to Florida every year. _____
14 The girl is reading the newspaper. _____
15 The children like milk very much. _____
16 Mr. Smith smokes many cigarettes. _____
17 The boys are sitting in the room now. _____
18 Mary often goes to the movies. _____
19 The men are fixing the car now. _____
20 The students are studying the lesson. _____

Exercise 54 Change these statements into negatives.

1 He is eating dinner now. *He isn't eating dinner now.*
2 We like coffee very much. _____
3 That student works very hard. _____
4 It is snowing outside now. _____
5 He spends much money every day. _____
6 Frank is talking to the teacher. _____
7 Mr. White speaks Spanish very well. _____
8 They are looking at the pictures now. _____
9 It rains very much in the winter. _____
10 I know many English words. _____
11 She is reading the newspaper right now. _____
12 They watch television every night of the week. _____
13 He is listening to the radio right now. _____
14 You are holding the box carefully. _____

43

Exercise 55 Use the correct present tense in each sentence.

SIMPLE: I work.   He studies.
CONTINUOUS: I am working.   He is studying.

1 He (like) sandwiches. _____
2 The men (fix) the car now. _____
3 The girl (speak) English very well. _____
4 I (owe) John fifty cents. _____
5 The women (be) from South America. _____
6 She (talk) to the teacher now. _____
7 It (rain) very much in this country. _____
8 The Browns often (attend) concerts. _____
9 The boys (open) the door now. _____
10 We always (go) to bed early. _____
11 The maid (prepare) dinner now. _____
12 Uncle John (eat) here every night. _____
13 John and Frank (write) letters right now. _____
14 Mary (need) some money. _____
15 The boys (study) for two hours every night. _____

(part two)

16 Mr. Smith (pay) many bills every month. _____
17 The children (be) very tired tonight. _____
18 The boy (run) into the building now. _____
19 The teacher (close) the door at nine o'clock. _____
20 Mrs. Williams (look) at the paper now. _____
21 Mr. Brown (teach) English from nine to eleven. ____
22 He (begin) the class right now. _____
23 Mr. Smith (fly) to California every winter. _____
24 Miss Williams (dance) very well. _____
25 He (watch) a baseball game every Saturday. _____
26 Mrs. Smith (talk) to Mr. Brown now. _____
27 They (come) here several times a week. _____
28 He (put) the boxes on the floor right now. _____
29 He (work) thirty-five hours a week. _____
30 She (know) all of the new words now. _____
31 They (finish) the work right now. _____
32 John (smile) at that pretty girl now. _____
33 We always (do) the lessons carefully. _____
34 We (do) lesson four right now. _____

44

Pages 34 - 44

all 36
attend 44
away 35
bank 36
baseball 37
be 44
bill 44
boat 38
bone 40
but 36
California 44
call 39
check 41
city 41
classroom 42
comfortable 37
concert 44
course 40
Cuba 42
dance 43
dinner 44
dog 40
each 43
early 37
eight 44
Elizabeth 42
enjoy 42
example 35
finish 37
Florida 43
funny 36
George 40
glass 41
grocery store 36
history 37
home 36
immediately 37

joke 36
late 42
laugh 42
leave 37
let's 36
light 40
like 34
maid 44
make 38
mirror 38
morning 37
month 44
move 41
next 37
often 37
once 42
owe 44
paper 40
pay 44
piano 41
please 35
prepare 44
Ralph 42
sandwich 44
San Francisco 42
sentence 36
shelf 42
side 42
similar 37
smoke 43
socks 41
someone 36
strong 38
sugar 38
suitcase 41
tea 41
ten 44

thousand 42
travel 43
tree 40
uncle 44
usually 37
water 40
wear 35
would 35
year 37
young 41

English is easy!

45

LESSON FIVE

5A The object pronouns

1	I	me	we	us
2	you	you	you	you
3	he she it	him her it	they	them

5B The object pronouns after verbs

Use the object forms of the pronouns directly after verbs.

The boy	likes	the girl
He	likes	her.

The girl	likes	the boy.
She	likes	him.

Charles knows the word.   OR   He knows it.
The boys like the books.   OR   They like them.
The girls study the lessons.   OR   They study them.

5C The object pronouns after prepositions

Use the object forms of the pronouns after prepositions.

Please speak	to	the man.
Please speak	to	him.

Please speak	to	the woman
Please speak	to	her.

at the joke   OR at it   for the boys   OR for them
to those men OR to them   from the girls OR from them

5D The words *much* and *many*, *a little* and *a few*

NOT COUNTABLE   COUNTABLE

much money   many dollars
much bread   many sandwiches
much coffee   many cups of coffee

a little water   a few glasses
a little bread   a few pieces of bread

Notice the difference between <u>much time</u> (hours, minutes,
etc.) and <u>many times</u> (occasions). The expressions <u>a little</u>
and <u>a few</u> do not usually occur in negative sentences.

5E The expressions *a lot of* and *lots of*

much	She	drinks	much	milk	every day.
or <u>a lot of</u>	She	drinks	a lot of	milk	every day.
or <u>lots of</u>	She	drinks	lots of	milk	every day.

many	He	eats	many	sandwiches	every day.
or <u>a lot of</u>	He	eats	a lot of	sandwiches	every day.
or <u>lots of</u>	He	eats	lots of	sandwiches	every day.

<u>A lot of</u> and <u>lots of</u> have the same meaning. These expressions are substitutes for both <u>much</u> and <u>many</u>. <u>A lot of</u> and <u>lots of</u> do not usually occur in negative sentences.

5F The words *very* and *too*

very hot	too hot
very fat	too fat
very many students	too many students
very much water	too much water

The word <u>too</u> means "excessively." The word <u>very</u> means "to a great extent or degree." The word <u>quite</u> means "to a certain extent or degree" or "somewhat." <u>Quite (hot)</u> and <u>rather (hot)</u> have the same meaning. <u>Quite a few (students)</u> has approximately the same meaning as <u>many (students)</u>. Substitute <u>very</u> for <u>quite</u> in questions and negatives. Substitute <u>many</u> for <u>quite a few</u> in questions and negatives.

5G The words *some* and *any*

Statement:	There is	some	milk on the table.
Question:	Is there	some / any	milk on the table?
Negative:	There isn't	any	milk on the table.

There are	some	students in the room.
Are there	some / any	students in the room?
There aren't	any	students in the room.

<u>Some</u> and <u>any</u> precede countable and uncountable nouns. <u>Some</u> occurs in statements and questions. <u>Any</u> occurs in questions and negatives. Temporarily, <u>any</u> is preferable in questions.

47

5H Frequency words

positive force   negative force

| always | frequently | | sometimes | seldom |
| usually | often | | occasionally | never |

Pay attention to the position of the frequency words in the following sentences.

Charles is	always	here after four o'clock.
Is Charles	always	here after four o'clock?
Charles isn't	always	here after four o'clock.

Charles		always	gets to school on time.
Does Charles		always	get to school on time ?
	Charles doesn't	always	get to school on time.

Exceptions: [1] The words frequently, usually, sometimes, and occasionally also occur at the beginning of the sentence (example: Sometimes we use that word in a different way.). [2] The expression very often also occurs at the end of the sentence (example: Our teacher gives us examinations very often.).

Note: Frequency words with negative force do not usually occur in questions and negatives.

Note: Ever replaces never in questions and negatives.

Frank is	never	there in the afternoon.
Is Frank	ever	there in the afternoon?
Frank isn't	ever	there in the afternoon.

Frank		never	gets to work on time.
Does Frank		ever	get to work on time?
	Frank doesn't	ever	get to work on time.

5J Idioms

all in all: All in all, the last lesson was not difficult for me.

and so forth (frequently written etc.): We need paper, pencils, pens, and so forth.

for instance: French words and English words are often similar. For instance, "leçon" is similar to "lesson."

keep up with: Are you keeping up with the other students?

look forward to: They are looking forward to their vacation.

look up: Please look up that new word in the dictionary.

make fun of: He frequently makes fun of my pronunciation.

make noise: The children are making too much noise now.

never mind: Do you want some help? -- Never mind. It's not important.

once and for all: Let's settle that matter once and for all!

odds and ends: I always keep odds and ends in that drawer.

on one hand On one hand, John likes that car very much .

on the other hand: But on the other hand, it's too expensive.

one another: John and Frank know one another very well.

pick out: Let's pick out a pretty red dress at that store.

pick up: Please pick up the wastepaper on the floor now.

play a joke (or trick) on: Frank is playing a joke on Tom. He often plays tricks on people.

quite a few: Are there many people in the room? -- Yes, there are quite a few people in the room now.

second-hand: Charles is looking for a second-hand car.

spend time on: Do you spend much time on the lessons?

throw away: Please throw away that wastepaper right now.

to some extent: To some extent, your statement is true.

up to date: That pretty black dress is very much up to date.

without doubt: Without doubt, you are right in that matter.

EXERCISES FOR LESSON FIVE

Exercise 56 Use isn't, aren't, don't, or doesn't.

1 This lesson *isn't* very difficult.   *isn't*
2 The students —— like American coffee.   _____
3 The children —— playing right now.   _____
4 John —— know the answer to the question.   _____
5 We —— listening to the radio now.   _____
6 The men —— from South America.   _____
7 He —— speak English very well.   _____
8 She —— keeping up with the class.   _____
9 Mr. Smith —— teach history.   _____
10 Alice and I —— very tired.   _____

Exercise 57 Use the correct present tense of each verb.

1 The sun (shine) now. _____ *The sun is shining now.*
2 The sun (get) very hot during the day. _____
3 Mary (play) the piano every evening. _____
4 Tom (look) forward to a vacation in June. _____
5 The children (sleep) every afternoon. _____
6 The student (look up) the word right now. _____
7 The boy (study) the lessons every day. _____
8 The women (put away) the dishes now. _____
9 The girl (read) an interesting book. _____
10 Alice (pick up) the wastepaper now. _____

Exercise 58 Use that, there, or what.

1 Is *that* man from Europe?   *that*
2 —— is he carrying?   _____
3 —— are lots of books on the shelf.   _____
4 Are —— many students in —— class?   _____
5 Is —— an overcoat?   _____
6 —— do you want?   _____
7 —— are a lot of chairs in —— room.   _____
8 —— are they doing now?   _____
9 Is —— boy reading —— book?   _____
10 —— is —— ?   _____

Exercise 59   Add <u>much</u>, <u>many</u>, or <u>very</u>.

1   The man is hungry. _____ *The man is very hungry.*
2   He drinks coffee every day. _____
3   John eats sandwiches every day. _____
4   These lessons take time. _____
5   I go there — times each week. _____
6   She isn't thirsty. _____
7   That boy is fat. _____
8   Are there people in the room? _____
9   Is she putting sugar in the coffee? _____
10 The weather in August is hot. _____
11 Does Mr. Brown have friends? _____
12 This is a straight road. _____
13 Are there girls in that class? _____
14 He lives in the big white house. _____
15 People wear hats. _____
16 These lessons are difficult. _____
17 Is there bread in the kitchen? _____
18 Is the Cuban student happy here? _____
19 English is an easy language. _____
20 The students are making noise now. _____

Exercise 60   Add <u>a little</u> or <u>a few</u>.

1   Mr. Smith has money. *Mr. Smith has a little money.*
2   He has friends here. _____
3   There is water in the bottle. _____
4   There are sandwiches on the table. _____
5   John is eating ice cream now. _____
6   There are students in the room. _____
7   There is fruit in the dish. _____
8   People are coming into the room. _____
9   There is butter on the plate. _____
10 I spend time on English each evening. _____
11 Guests are always late. _____
12 I have cigarettes left. _____
13 I have money in the bank. _____
14 There are books on the floor. _____
15 She is putting bread on the table. _____

Exercise 61 Change <u>much</u> or <u>many</u> to <u>a lot of</u>.

1 He has much money. _____ *He has a lot of money.*
2 The students know many songs. _____
3 Much sugar comes from Cuba. _____
4 There is much milk on the table. _____
5 There are many people here now. _____
6 The boy is eating much ice cream. _____
7 There is much bread in the kitchen. _____
8 There are many students in the room. _____
9 He is putting much cream in the coffee. _____
10 The Spanish student has many friends. _____
11 Many people enjoy television each night. _____
12 Mr. Smith drinks much coffee each day. _____
13 I have much trouble with the short words. _____
14 There are many short words in English. _____
15 Frank receives many letters every day. _____
16 Many people speak the English language. _____
17 I have many friends at that school. _____
18 We learn many new words every day. _____

Exercise 62 Use the sentences in exercise sixty-one.
Change <u>much</u> or <u>many</u> to <u>lots of</u>.

1 He has much money. _____ *He has lots of money.*

Exercise 63 Use <u>too</u>, <u>too much</u>, or <u>too many</u>.

1	*too* warm	6	____ dollars	11	____ short
2	____ money	7	____ children	12	____ time
3	____ students	8	____ work	13	____ days
4	____ people	9	____ big	14	____ wide
5	____ rain	10	____ cake	15	____ weak

Exercise 64 Use <u>very</u>, <u>very little</u>, or <u>very few</u>.

1	*very few* students	6	____ money	11	____ fat
2	____ cold	7	____ time	12	____ work
3	____ sugar	8	____ times	13	____ coffee
4	____ hot	9	____ people	14	____ books
5	____ friends	10	____ happy	15	____ milk

Exercise 65 Add <u>too</u>, <u>too much</u>, or <u>too many</u>.

1 He eats ice cream. ____*He eats too much ice cream*.
2 Mr. Brown has money. _____
3 He has friends. _____
4 It is cold today. _____
5 The car is long. _____
6 The students are making noise. _____
7 He is putting sugar in the coffee. _____
8 There are pictures on the wall. _____
9 We hear music on the radio. _____
10 There is milk in the glass. _____
11 The exercises take time. _____
12 The exercises are easy. _____

Exercise 66 Use <u>some</u> or <u>any</u> in each blank space.

1 We don't have _*any*_ money. *any*
2 They don't want ____ coffee.
3 The boys want ____ dessert now.
4 John is eating ____ ice cream now.
5 He doesn't want ____ sugar in the coffee.
6 There aren't ____ chairs in that room.
7 There are ____ paintings on the wall.
8 I don't know ____ words in Persian.
9 She doesn't want ____ dessert after dinner.
10 He's putting ____ salt and pepper on the table.
11 I don't have ____ time right now.
12 Do you know ____ new songs?

Exercise 67 Change these statements into negatives.

1 He needs some money. ____*He doesn't need any money*.
2 She is eating some candy. _____
3 They have some money now. _____
4 There's some milk on the table. _____
5 There are some sandwiches here. _____
6 Mr. Brown knows some Persian. _____
7 There's some paper in the notebook. _____
8 The men want some coffee now. _____
9 He's putting some sugar in the coffee. _____
10 There are some students in that room. _____

Exercise 68 Reverse the subject and the object.

1	We know her. _She knows us._	11	He knows her. _____
2	They know us. _We know them._	12	You know them. _____
3	She knows him. _____	13	We know you. _____
4	I know you. _____	14	She knows them. _____
5	He knows them. _____	15	They know him. _____
6	You know me. _____	16	I know her. _____
7	We know him. _____	17	He knows me. _____
8	She knows us. _____	18	You know him. _____
9	They know you. _____	19	We know them. _____
10	I know him. _____	20	They know her. _____

Exercise 69 Substitute pronouns for the underlined words.

1 Do you like this school? _____ _Do you like it?_
2 John is hitting the ball now. _____
3 He knows Mr. Smith very well. _____
4 Do you see those new cars? _____
5 I do not hear the children. _____
6 Do you know Miss Smith? _____
7 We are helping mother now. _____
8 Is he speaking to Mr. Adams? _____
9 Do you know those men? _____
10 I am helping John with the lesson. _____
11 We are getting help from Miss Brown. _____
12 I don't like this candy very much. _____
13 He is writing the letters now. _____
14 Does he know Mr. and Mrs. Smith? _____
15 I send a letter to Helen and Betty every week. _____
16 The students like Miss Brown. _____
17 She's putting the food on the table. _____
18 John is answering the question correctly. _____
19 He buys cigarettes at the corner store. _____
20 Do they know that woman very well? _____
21 The boys are moving the chairs into the room. _____
22 Do you enjoy television very much? _____
23 Does John know the new students? _____
24 The boy is giving the box to the men. _____
25 The teacher is reading the story to the students. _____

Exercise 70   Follow the example.

1   Is he helping you?   Yes, but ___*I'm not helping him.*___
2   Are you helping them?   Yes, but ___*they aren't*___ -- --
3   Am I helping you?   Yes, but _____
4   Are they helping her?   Yes, but _____
5   Are you helping him?   Yes, but _____
6   Is she helping you?   Yes, but _____
7   Are they helping him?   Yes, but _____
8   Is he helping her?   Yes, but _____
9   Are they helping you?   Yes, but _____
10 Am I helping him?   Yes, but _____

Exercise 71   Substitute pronouns for the underlined words.

1   The chair is comfortable. ___*It is comfortable.*___
2   The tables are quite big. ___*They are quite big.*___
3   That blouse is very pretty. _____
4   The work isn't very hard. _____
5   This furniture is expensive. _____
6   The boy is reading the book now. _____
7   Mary is walking to school with John. _____
8   The teachers are talking to the students. _____
9   The children like Miss Smith very much. _____
10 Does that student know the answer? _____
11 The women are answering the questions. _____
12 Does Mr. Smith know that man very well? _____
13 Miss Smith is explaining the lesson to the students. __
14 The child is playing with the toy. _____
15 The boys are putting things in the box. _____
16 John and Frank are writing the letter now. _____
17 The students like Mr. Brown very much. _____
18 The man understands the lesson very well. _____
19 Do Charles and Mary like that book? _____
20 Are the men speaking to Mary and Helen? _____
21 Is the woman writing in the notebook? _____
22 The children are playing with the dog. _____
23 Is Miss Brown giving the books to the man? _____
24 The people don't like the news very much. _____
25 Mrs. Brown is reading the lesson to the students. __

55

Exercise 72   Add <u>ever</u> or <u>never</u>.

1 I eat there. _____ *I never eat there.*
2 That student is on time. _____
3 They don't speak to us. _____
4 Do you make fun of people? _____
5 She doesn't save odds and ends. _____
6 The clothes in that store are up to date. _____
7 John studies very hard. _____
8 Does he drink much coffee? _____
9 The coffee at this cafeteria is good. _____
10 The sandwiches aren't expensive. _____

Exercise 73   Add the indicated words.

(part one)

1 (always) That student is late. *That student is always late.*
2 (seldom) Tom eats toast for breakfast. _____
3 (often) The children are very noisy. _____
4 (usually) Mr. Smith walks to work. _____
5 (seldom) John drinks milk at lunch. _____
6 (never) That man works very hard. _____
7 (usually) Are the lessons interesting? _____
8 (always) Does he come here at 9:00 a.m.? _____
9 (often) The lessons aren't difficult. _____
10 (usually) The water isn't cold. _____

(part two)

11 (always) Is there enough food in the refrigerator? _____
12 (usually) Do you study the lessons at night? _____
13 (seldom) We listen to the radio during the day. _____
14 (often) The men are very busy. _____
15 (sometimes) I write with a ballpoint pen. _____
16 (frequently) We are at home in the evening. _____
17 (always) Do they repeat the sentences word for word? _
18 (usually) Is it cold in the fall? _____
19 (ever) They don't practice the sentences. _____
20 (always) Are the dishes on that shelf? _____

Exercise 74   Complete these idioms.

(part one)

1	Let's buy a —— hand car.	*second-hand*
2	The two men know —— another very well.	_____
3	I always say the words —— and over.	_____
4	All —— all, I enjoy that class.	_____
5	He's looking —— that name in the telephone book.	_____
6	We spend a lot of time —— new words.	_____
7	Don't make fun —— that student!	_____
8	I agree with him —— some extent.	_____
9	—— doubt, he knows the answer.	_____
10	First —— all, let's ask the teacher.	_____
11	Is that car —— sale?	_____
12	Look —— ! You're driving too fast!	_____
13	He usually wakes —— quite early.	_____
14	Does he always get —— right away?	_____
15	It's easy. —— instance, this sentence is on page forty-nine.	_____

(part two)

16	Let's decide that once and —— all.	_____
17	We always repeat the sentences word —— word.	_____
18	—— one hand, it's interesting.	_____
19	But —— the other hand, it's difficult.	_____
20	William enjoys a movie —— and then.	_____
21	Let's take a —— to Canada next summer.	_____
22	Do you always go —— bed at the same time?	_____
23	He often plays tricks —— us.	_____
24	There are quite —— few exercises in the book.	_____
25	It's hot! Let's go —— a walk.	_____
26	Would you please sit —— in that easy chair.	_____
27	Is this telephone book up —— date?	_____
28	She's picking —— the paper on the floor.	_____
29	There are three suits. Let's pick —— one.	_____
30	Please bring paper, pencils, and —— forth.	_____
31	Never —— . That's not important.	_____
32	Are you keeping —— with the other students?	_____

57

VOCABULARY FOR LESSON FIVE

Pages 46 - 57

agree 57
Alice 49
always 48
a.m. 56
any 47
August 51
ballpoint pen 56
Betty 54
bottle 51
bread 51
butter 51
cafeteria 56
cake 52
Canada 57
corner 54
correctly 54
cream 52
Cuban 51
dessert 53
dictionary 49
dollar 46
drive 57
during 56
easy chair 57
enough 56
ever 48
fall 56
fat 51
few 46
food 54
frequently 48
fruit 51
furniture 55
guest 51
handkerchief 50
help 54

her 46
him 46
ice cream 51
important 49
June 50
keep 49
kitchen 51
left 51
little 46
lot 47
lots 47
lunch 56
me 46
mother 54
name 57
never 48
night 56
occasionally 48
o'clock 56
office 57
painting 53
pepper 53
Persian 53
plate 51
practice 49
refrigerator 56
right 49
road 51
salt 53
same 57
say 49
seldom 48
short 52
song 52
sometimes 48
straight 51

summer 57
them 46
thing 55
thirsty 51
time 46
times 51
toast 56
too 47
true 49
us 46
vacation 49
warm 52
weak 52
wide 52

English is easy! You don't practice enough.

That's not true!

Gentlemen! Please don't argue!

58

LESSON SIX

6A   The past tense of be

	present	past
1	I am	I was
2	you are	you were
3	he she is it	he she was it

present	past
we are	we were
you are	you were
they are	they were

Examples:

I was at home yesterday.
John was there last night.
It was hot yesterday.
There was a man here.

They were absent yesterday.
She was a student last year.
We were here last week.
There were some men here.

6B   Statements, questions, and negatives

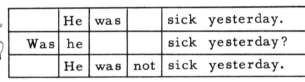

Statement:		He	was		sick yesterday.
Question:	Was	he			sick yesterday?
Negative:		He	was	not	sick yesterday.

6C   The past tense of regular verbs

The past tense expresses a completed action at a definite time in the past.

Simple present:	We	work	hard every day.
Past:	We	worked	hard yesterday.

All subject pronouns require the same past tense form:

I worked, you worked, he worked, they worked, etc.

6D   Spelling the past tense forms of regular verbs

learn	live	study	stop
learned	lived	studied	stopped

59

Examples:

(1) need, needed; seem, seemed; want, wanted
(2) move, moved; smoke, smoked; agree, agreed
(3) try, tried; cry, cried; marry, married
(4) slip, slipped; permit, permitted; admit, admitted

6E Statements, questions, and negatives

The past tense of <u>do</u> and <u>does</u> = <u>did</u>.

	They			walked	to school yesterday.
Did	they			walk	to school yesterday?
	They	did	not	walk	to school yesterday.
	He			studied	the lesson last night.
Did	he			study	the lesson last night?
	He	did	not	study	the lesson last night.

6F Contractions with *was, were,* and *did*

was	not	=	wasn't
were	not	=	weren't

did not = didn't

6G Time expressions with the past tense

YESTERDAY   yesterday morning, yesterday afternoon

LAST ----   last night, last Tuesday, last Tuesday morning, last week, last June, last June 15, last spring, last month, last year

---- AGO   a moment ago, a few minutes ago, a day ago, two days ago, a week ago, a month ago, a year ago a week ago yesterday, a week ago Saturday

--- BEFORE ---   the day before yesterday (the day before last), the week before last, the month before last

6H The prepositions *by* and *with*

BY   (1) method:

        We go to school by bus every day.
        They traveled to Europe by plane.
        She makes her dresses by hand.

      (2) the meaning "near" :

        The library is by the post office.
        The bus stops by the store on the corner.

WITH   (1) accompaniment:

        John walked into the room with Tom.
        They studied the lesson with us last night.

      (2) means or instrument:

        Mr. Adams writes with his left hand.
        He is taking some pictures with the new camera.

6J Idioms

by hand: Those girls make all of their dresses by hand.

by mistake: Did Charles do the wrong lesson by mistake?

do the dishes: We did the dishes after dinner last night.

do the lesson: I do the new lesson every day.   Did you do
the last lesson?   He didn't do that lesson very carefully.

do the work: Did the students do all of the work carefully?

know by heart: Do you know the new verbs by heart now?

learn by heart: Did you learn all of the words by heart?

take a trip: Mr. Adams takes a long trip every summer.

the last straw: That's the last straw.   Stop it at once!

turn around: Charles turned around and walked in the other
direction.   He turned the car around in the street.

turn over: He turned over the pages of the books slowly.
Did the other car turn over at the time of the accident?

EXERCISES FOR LESSON SIX

Exercise 75   Supply a different verb in each sentence.

1   Please _read_ the book.   _read_
2   Would you please ——— these words.   ———
3   Please ——— that door.   ———
4   Would you please ——— to the teacher.   ———
5   Please ——— the book to Mr. Smith.   ———
6   Would you please ——— the window.   ———
7   Please ——— the light.   ———
8   Would you please ——— the sandwiches.   ———
9   Would you ——— the question, please.   ———
10 Please ——— the assignment.   ———

Exercise 76   Use <u>a</u>, <u>an</u>, <u>some</u>, or <u>any</u>.

1   This is _a_ very old building.   _a_
2   He is carrying ——— things in that box.   ———
3   The boy from Colombia is ——— student here.   ———
4   Mr. Stevens always carries ——— umbrella.   ———
5   There isn't ——— new furniture in this room.   ———
6   Mr. Brown has ——— new typewriter.   ———
7   He didn't want ——— cream in his coffee.   ———
8   John always eats ——— egg for breakfast.   ———
9   He usually has ——— coffee afterwards.   ———
10 He frequently takes ——— sandwiches to school.   ———

Exercise 77   Choose the correct word for each sentence.

1   That is (a, an) very old book.   _a_
2   Are there (much, many) farms in this country?   ———
3   John is carrying (some, any) furniture now.   ———
4   That boy (never, ever) prepares for this class.   ———
5   The weather is often (too, too much) hot there.   ———
6   Do you speak (much, many) English?   ———
7   You don't (never, ever) answer questions.   ———
8   She isn't preparing (some, any) meat for dinner.   ———
9   There are (too, too many) people in this room.   ———
10 He doesn't (never, ever) come to class on time.   ———

62

Exercise 78   Change each verb to the past tense.

(part one)

1   We are happy. _____ *We were happy.*
2   That road is smooth. _____
3   The news is a great surprise. _____
4   I am very sleepy. _____
5   They are in the office now. _____

(part two)

6   Is the sandwich good? _____
7   Am I right or wrong? _____
8   Is there any food in the refrigerator? _____
9   Are you happy about the news? _____
10 Are there many students in that class? _____

(part three)

11 They aren't in the other room. _____
12 The crowd isn't very large. _____
13 I'm not familiar with that word. _____
14 There aren't enough glasses on the table. _____
15 The bottle isn't full. _____

Exercise 79   Change each verb to the past tense.

1   We attend many lectures. *We attended many lectures.*
2   I prepare each lesson carefully. _____
3   She dances very well. _____
4   They enjoy it very much. _____
5   Mr. Stevens owes me fifty dollars. _____

6   Do you finish at six o'clock? _____
7   Does he like it very much? _____
8   Do they practice the new words? _____
9   Does it seem cold? _____
10 Does Miss Adams help you with the lessons? _____

11 She doesn't agree with me. _____
12 I don't like it at all. _____
13 Mrs. Williams doesn't prepare dinner early. _____
14 Tom and Bill don't study every night. _____
15 He doesn't work for that company. _____

Exercise 80 Write <u>was</u> or <u>were</u> in each blank space.

1 He <u>was</u> in the library this morning.   *was*
2 I —— quite tired last night.   _____
3 The boy —— at school yesterday.   _____
4 The sun —— hot yesterday.   _____
5 Mr. Smith —— sick two days ago.   _____
6 The weather —— good last week.   _____
7 The children —— here yesterday.   _____
8 The boys —— at the meeting last night.   _____
9 It —— very warm yesterday.   _____
10 There —— a fire downtown last night.   _____

Exercise 81 Change these statements into questions.

1 He was in class yesterday. *Was he in class yesterday?*
2 They were here last night. _____
3 The doctor was very tired. _____
4 There were many people at the party. _____
5 There was a party here last night. _____
6 It was very interesting. _____
7 John was sick last week. _____
8 John and Mary were here yesterday. _____
9 They were at the meeting last night. _____
10 It was warm yesterday. _____

Exercise 82 Change these statements into negatives.

1 The men were in the room. *The men weren't in the room.*
2 You were there yesterday. _____
3 The boy from Chile was there. _____
4 There were some chairs in the room. _____
5 It was very cold last night. _____
6 John was absent from class yesterday. _____
7 He was in California last winter. _____
8 There was a big celebration afterwards. _____
9 It was a very good football game. _____
10 The people were very happy. _____
11 The weather was good. _____
12 There was enough food. _____

Exercise 83 Write the correct past tense form of each verb in the following blank space.

1 (study) John *studied* French last year.   *studied*
2 (live) They —— in New York for one year.   ——
3 (walk) Mr. Smith —— in the park last Sunday.   ——
4 (watch) We —— a baseball game on television.   ——
5 (smoke) I —— two cigars yesterday.   ——
6 (wash) Mrs. Smith —— the clothes last Monday.   ——
7 (like) Bob —— the movie last night.   ——
8 (stop) The car —— in the middle of Main Street.   ——
9 (listen) We —— to the radio last night.   ——
10 (rain) It —— very hard the night before last.   ——

Exercise 84 Change these statements into questions:

1 He worked at the office. *Did he work at the office ?*
2 She opened the door carefully. ————
3 They looked at the pictures. ————
4 John asked many questions in class. ————
5 Mr. Smith added the numbers carefully. ————
6 Mr. and Mrs. Brown invited the students. ————
7 You lived in Miami for a year. ————
8 The men moved the furniture into the room. ————
9 The girls visited Mrs. Smith last week. ————
10 You worked very hard yesterday. ————

Exercise 85 Change these statements into negatives.

1 I looked at the pictures. *I didn't look at the pictures.*
2 They counted the money carefully. ————
3 We needed some money last week. ————
4 They watched the baseball game yesterday. ————
5 John carried the box into the room. ————
6 Mr. Smith wanted some coffee. ————
7 The students used the book last night. ————
8 The Chinese student listened to the teacher. ————
9 He repeated the question for the student. ————
10 Mary played the piano at the party. ————
11 The boys studied the lesson carefully. ————
12 John answered all of the questions. ————

65

Exercise 86 Change these statements to questions.

1 The bank is near the library. *Is the bank near the library?*
2 The class begins at 10:30 a.m. _____
3 He asked for the address of the company. _____
4 I borrowed the money from him. _____
5 That house belongs to Mr. Williams. _____
6 Mr. and Mrs. Brown own the other one. _____
7 The people were here at eight o'clock. _____
8 The clerk counted the money carefully. _____
9 There were several coats in the closet. _____
10 He asked that cute girl for a date. _____
11 It was cool here yesterday. _____
12 The boys carried the furniture carefully. _____
13 The furniture is new. _____
14 I know all of the words by heart. _____
15 The bottle on the shelf was empty. _____
16 The instructor explained the lesson. _____
17 Tom is doing the lesson now. _____
18 That hotel has good food. _____
19 There is a nice restaurant in the next block. _____
20 We practiced the new words last night. _____

Exercise 87 Change these statements to negatives.

1 The teacher is very strict. *The teacher isn't very strict.*
2 We liked the movie very much. _____
3 They received a reply on Tuesday. _____
4 He is wearing a cotton shirt. _____
5 We finished the work on time. _____
6 There were many sandwiches on the plate. _____
7 She remembered the name of the song. _____
8 Spring is always a pleasant season. _____
9 That store sells expensive clothes. _____
10 I noticed the traffic sign. _____
11 It was very warm yesterday. _____
12 They take a long trip every summer. _____
13 They are listening to the radio now. _____
14 He turned around quickly. _____
15 We always do the dishes after dinner. _____

66

Exercise 88 Make contractions if possible.

1 I did not go.
2 He was not there.
3 They were not here.
4 You were not there.
5 It was not cold.
6 It did not rain.
7 We were not angry.
8 We did not see it.
9 I was not absent.
10 They were not here.
11 It did not come.
12 It was not warm.
13 They were not angry.
14 She was not at school.
15 He did not go there.
16 It was not interesting.
17 They did not know it.
18 We were not absent.
19 She was not late.
20 There was not any milk.
21 It did not rain.
22 It was not cold.
23 She did not like it.
24 We were not ready.
25 It was not pretty.
26 We did not know it.
27 You were not here.
28 I did not see it.
29 That was not right.
30 I was not ready.
31 She did not come.
32 We were not angry.
33 He did not like it.
34 You did not go.
35 She was not absent.
36 They were not ready.
37 She did not come back.
38 I was not sick.

Exercise 89 Make contractions if possible.

1 She is not a teacher.
2 I am very busy now.
3 They did not go.
4 He does not like it.
5 She is a student.
6 John was not ready.
7 I am not a student.
8 They do not know it.
9 We are very happy.
10 It is very hot now.
11 He was not late.
12 What is that?
13 There is a man here.
14 That is a nice house.
15 It did not rain hard.
16 It was not very good.
17 She is not here now.
18 It is not ready yet.
19 That is a sweater.
20 There is not any here.
21 What is this?
22 He does not know it.
23 She is not ready.
24 They were not angry.
25 You did not come.
26 I do not see it.
27 It was not difficult.
28 There is a man here.
29 That is very good.
30 She is not ready.
31 There is a book here.
32 It is very pretty.
33 I am ready now.
34 He was wrong.
35 They were not here.
36 That is interesting.
37 I am not a doctor.
38 It was very pretty.

Exercise 90 Write <u>yesterday</u>, <u>last</u>, or <u>ago</u> in the blank space in each sentence.

1   We were at the party *last* night.
2   Did you visit them ——week?
3   Were there many people here —— Wednesday?
4   They arrived about an hour ——.
5   Were Tom and Charles in New York a year——.
6   Miss White was in Italy —— year.
7   Did you study in the library——afternoon?
8   We received a letter from him several days——.
9   Was Bill in class —— morning?
10 There were some visitors here the week before ——.
11 I studied for two hours —— night.
12 Were you at home ——?
13 It was very cold here —— winter.
14 Did they finish the work —— night?
15 I was there a long time ——.
16 The instructor explained the lesson to us ——.
17 Did you borrow the money —— month?
18 We visited Aunt Martha —— weekend.
19 They were in South America the year before ——.
20 Was he absent from class ——?

Exercise 91 Write <u>by</u> or <u>with</u> in the blank space in each sentence.

1   We traveled to Japan _by_ boat.   _by_
2   Did you travel —— the other students?   ————
3   I studied the wrong lesson —— mistake.   ————
4   Do you write —— a pencil or a pen?   ————
5   Do you usually study —— John?   ————
6   Did he learn the words ——heart?   ————
7   I usually go to school —— bus.   ————
8   Do you write ——your right hand?   ————
9   The boy is hitting the baseball —— a bat.   ————
10 Let's go downtown —— car.   ————
11 I often eat lunch —— John and Bill.   ————
12 She is making the dress —— hand.   ————
13 They didn't go there____car.   ————
14 We usually eat soup____ a spoon.   ————
15 Many people in New York travel___subway.   ————

VOCABULARY FOR LESSON SIX

Pages 59 - 68

absent 59
add 65
after 61
afterwards 62
ago 60
arrive 68
assignment 62
aunt 68
bat 68
before 60
belong 66
block 66
borrow 66
celebration 64
Chile 64
Chinese 65
closet 66
clothes 65
Colombia 62
company 63
cool 66
cotton 66
country 62
cute 66
didn't 60
direction 61
downtown 64
empty 66
explain 66
familiar 63
farm 62
fire 64
football 64
full 63
great 63
hotel 66

invite 65
last 59
lecture 63
main 65
Martha 68
meat 62
meeting 64
Miami 65
middle 65
minute 60
moment 60
Monday 65
near 66
notice 66
number 65
or 63
outside 62
own 66
plane 60
quickly 66
remember 66
restaurant 66
season 66
sell 66
sign 66
sleepy 63
slip 59
slowly 61
smooth 63
soup 68
spoon 68
spring 60
Stevens 62
street 65
subway 68
Sunday 65

surprise 63
sweater 67
traffic 66
trip 66
Tuesday 60
typewriter 62
university 64
use 65
verb 61
visitor 68
was 59
wasn't 60
Wednesday 68
were 59
weren't 60
winter 64
wrong 61
yesterday 59

English is easy! Don't forget that!

Yes, sir. No, sir.

69

LESSON SEVEN

7A   The past tense of irregular verbs

The irregular verb DRINK :

Simple present:	He	drinks	much water every day.
Past:	He	drank	much water yesterday.

[I drank, you drank, they drank, etc.]

7B   Statements, questions, and negatives

The irregular verb EAT :

	The boys		ate	many sandwiches last night.
Did	the boys		eat	many sandwiches last night ?
	The boys	did not	eat	many sandwiches last night.

7C   The irregular verbs (part one)

present	past	present	past
am, is, are	was, were	leave	left
bring	brought	put	put
build	built	read	read
buy	bought	ride	rode
choose	chose	ring	rang
do	did	say	said
drink	drank	see	saw
drive	drove	sell	sold
eat	ate	send	sent
feel	felt	shut	shut
find	found	sing	sang
fly	flew	sleep	slept
forgive	forgave	speak	spoke
give	gave	spend	spent
go	went	take	took
grow	grew	teach	taught
hear	heard	tell	told
hit	hit	wake up	woke up
hurt	hurt	wear	wore
know	knew	write	wrote

These verbs are important.

70

7D In, on, and at in expressions of place

IN	ON	AT
in the world	on Fifth Avenue	at 224 Fifth Avenue
in Europe	on Cherry Street	at 61 Cherry Street
in California	on the corner (of)	at the corner (of)
in Brooklyn	on Long Island	at the intersection
in Boston	on the floor	at the Lincoln Hotel
in the park	on the third floor	at Times Square
in the street	on the wall	at New York University
in the car	on the sidewalk	at Dartmouth College
in the driveway	on the subway	at the store
in the house	on the bus	at the airport
in the room	on the boat	at the station
in the drawer	on the (air)plane	at the concert
in the box	on the shelf	at the meeting
in the sky	on the table	at the door
in the water	on the radio	at home
in the third row	on television	at school
in the seat	on the sofa	at work
in the book	on the page	

7E Direct and indirect objects

These two sentences say the same thing. Both are correct.

Type (1)	The girl is giving		the book	to him.
Type (2)	The girl is giving	him	the book.	

The word to does not occur in type (2) sentences. In type (1) sentences, the indirect object follows the direct object. In type (2) sentences, the indirect object precedes the direct object. Use either type (1) or type (2) with the following verbs: bring, give, hand, lend, mail, offer, owe, pay, read, sell, send, show, teach, tell, throw, write.

Note: If the direct object is a pronoun, use only type (1):

My friend gave ⬚ it ⬚ to me last week.
Mr. Davis sent ⬚ them ⬚ to us yesterday.

Note: Use only type (1) with these verbs: describe, explain, introduce, mention, prove, report, return, say, suggest.

7F Idioms

at any rate: Someone took my pocketbook. -- Well, at any
rate, you still have your money.

at first: At first, I had a lot of trouble with this language.

at present: We are studying the irregular verbs at present.

at school (church, work, etc.):   The boys are at school
now.   Is he at work now?   The girls are at church now.

at the end of: We are usually tired at the end of the day.

go to school (church, work, etc.):   She goes to school five
days a week.   We go to church on Sunday.   Do you go to
work at 9:00 a.m. every day?

have lunch (dinner, etc.):   Do you usually have lunch with
Charles and Tom?   Mr. Brown has dinner at five-thirty.

in addition: Please write this lesson.   In addition, study
all of the new words.   In addition to that, read this page.

in a row: Mr. Adams drank three cups of coffee in a row.

in back of: There is a large garage in back of the house.

in fact: The fire was very bad.   In fact, it destroyed
several buildings.   - Yes, I liked it.   In fact, I bought it.

in front of: There is a large yard in front of the house.

in some respects (or ways): English is easy in some ways.
In some respects, the English language is quite difficult.

on purpose: Did those two students do that on purpose?

on second thought: On second thought, maybe you are right.

on the contrary: I don't hate it.   On the contrary, I like it.

on the whole: That was an interesting book on the whole.
On the whole, we enjoyed that radio program last night.

send... by airmail: He sent the letter to them by airmail.

take care of: Please take care of the baby for a minute.

tell a lie (joke, story, etc.):   He told us a lie about that.
Did Charles tell you a joke?   She told us a funny story.

tell the truth: Please tell us the truth about the accident.

Exercise 92 Change the underlined verbs to the past tense.

1 She <u>feels</u> fine. _____ *She felt fine.*
2 He <u>drinks</u> a lot of milk. _____
3 She <u>wears</u> very pretty clothes. _____
4 We <u>read</u> many magazines. _____
5 Tom <u>leaves</u> the office at five o'clock. _____
6 He <u>rides</u> to work with Bill. _____
7 The Smiths <u>buy</u> groceries at that store. _____
8 I <u>see</u> Tom in that room. _____
9 Mr. Brown <u>teaches</u> history and English. _____
10 I <u>hear</u> an airplane. _____

Exercise 93 Change the underlined verbs to the past tense.

1 <u>Does</u> she speak English? _____ *Did she speak English?*
2 <u>Does</u> he spend a lot of money? _____
3 <u>Do</u> you send many letters to her? _____
4 <u>Does</u> he write many letters to you? _____
5 <u>Does</u> Mr. Adams drive carefully? _____
6 <u>Do</u> they go there in the morning? _____
7 <u>Does</u> Tom eat at the cafeteria? _____
8 <u>Do</u> you feel all right? _____
9 <u>Does</u> the teacher give big assignments? _____
10 <u>Do</u> you sleep late in the morning? _____

Exercise 94 Change the underlined verbs to the past tense.

1 We <u>don't</u> eat there. _____ *We didn't eat there.*
2 Bill <u>doesn't</u> sing very well. _____
3 You <u>don't</u> tell us the answers. _____
4 She <u>doesn't</u> know the name of the book. _____
5 Ralph <u>doesn't</u> take English lessons. _____
6 I <u>don't</u> bring a dictionary to class. _____
7 We <u>don't</u> drive to school. _____
8 Miss Brown <u>doesn't</u> leave early. _____
9 They <u>don't</u> read many books. _____
10 Mr. White <u>doesn't</u> teach this class. _____
11 He <u>doesn't</u> drive very carefully. _____
12 Mary <u>doesn't</u> like that class. _____

Exercise 95   Write the past tense form of each verb.

(part one)

1   He (go) to a museum. _____ *He went to a museum.*
2   We (drive) to church this morning. _____
3   John (know) the answers to the questions. _____
4   The students (shut) the back door an hour ago. _____
5   He (come) to class late yesterday. _____
6   Mrs. Brown (wear) a new suit to the party. _____
7   Mr. Smith (buy) a new overcoat last week. _____
8   I (write) several letters last night. _____
9   They (take) a course in French last year. _____
10 Mr. Smith (teach) history last semester. _____
11 The students (read) the assignment carefully. _____
12 We (find) a purse on the chair. _____
13 She (choose) a pretty dress for the party. _____
14 The Chinese boy (bring) a friend to the party. _____
15 I (eat) three sandwiches at lunch today. _____

(part two)

16 She (send) the letter by airmail. _____
17 The French students (sing) some good songs. _____
18 Charles (feel) very bad yesterday. _____
19 He (drink) too much coffee last night. _____
20 The man (sell) the house at a low price. _____
21 I (sleep) for twelve hours last night. _____
22 That tree (grow) five feet last year. _____
23 The Browns (build) a new house last summer. _____
24 John (speak) to the teacher about it. _____
25 The teacher (tell) the students the answer. _____
26 I (ride) to school by bus this morning. _____
27 Mr. Smith (put) the umbrella beside the desk. _____
28 Charles (leave) for California two days ago. _____
29 The boy (hit) the ball over the wall. _____
30 She (spend) eighteen dollars over the weekend. _____
31 He (wear) a new suit yesterday. _____
32 They (go) to work early this morning. _____
33 Mr. Smith (teach) that class last year. _____
34 John (drive) the car very carefully. _____
35 The girls (buy) several new dresses. _____

Exercise 96 Change these statements to questions.

1 He sold the car. _____ *Did he sell the car?*
2 John bought a new pair of shoes. _____
3 He spoke to the boy after class. _____
4 She said some interesting things. _____
5 They went to the baseball game. _____
6 She brought a friend to school. _____
7 Mr. Brown wore a winter overcoat. _____
8 The students came at 8:00 a.m. _____
9 He made a mistake on the test. _____
10 The boys held the box carefully. _____
11 Frank wrote the answer on the paper. _____
12 John and Charles ate some sandwiches. _____
13 You drank too much coffee last night. _____
14 They felt very bad this morning. _____
15 The train left at 5:30 p.m. _____
16 Mary chose a pretty skirt. _____
17 Mr. Smith taught English last year. _____
18 Tom put the money in his billfold. _____
19 We found the purse on the floor. _____
20 They heard that radio program. _____

Exercise 97 Change these statements to negatives.

1 He ate a good meal. _____ *He didn't eat a good meal.*
2 She went to the movies last night. _____
3 He spoke to the teacher this morning. _____
4 The students knew the answers. _____
5 Mr. Smith sent the letter last night. _____
6 She put the book on the desk. _____
7 I wrote the word very carefully. _____
8 We saw some interesting buildings. _____
9 They read the lesson last night. _____
10 I brought some books to school. _____
11 We heard the new song. _____
12 John wore a new suit last night. _____
13 The Browns flew to Venezuela last year. _____
14 Charles gave me some money. _____
15 The two boys came to class late. _____

Exercise 98 Change the position of the direct object.

1 He gave the box to me. _____ *He gave me the box.*
2 Mr. Smith sent a letter to them. _____
3 We gave a birthday present to him. _____
4 She brought the books to them. _____
5 Tom handed the newspaper to her. _____
6 Did Charles throw the ball to Tom? _____
7 Mrs. Brown sent some flowers to me. _____
8 He sold the house to Mr. Smith. _____
9 The teacher read the story to us. _____
10 Mr. Brown wrote a letter to his son. _____

Exercise 99 Change the position of the direct object.

1 He gave her the book. _____ *He gave the book to her.*
2 We sent Mary a birthday present. _____
3 He gave the girl a gift. _____
4 John sold me the car yesterday. _____
5 Mrs. Smith gave Helen the box. _____
6 Frank gave Charles the tickets. _____
7 He showed Mr. Smith the photographs. _____
8 She told us an interesting story. _____
9 Mr. Brown mailed us a gift from Mexico. _____
10 Did John lend his brother ten dollars? _____

Exercise 100 Add the indicated expressions to the following sentences. Do not add any other words.

to him	1	I mailed it. _____ *I mailed it to him.*
him	2	They sold the house last week. _____
to me	3	Charles wrote a long letter. _____
me	4	Tom told a very funny joke. _____
you	5	Did they send a present? _____
to you	6	Did she return the money? _____
them	7	The instructor read the story. _____
to them	8	Did he explain it? _____
to her	9	I mailed the letter yesterday. _____
her	10	He told the truth. _____

Exercise 101   Use <u>in</u>, <u>on</u>, or <u>at</u>.

1   They live_____North Lincoln Street.   _____
2   Mr Brown was____ Cuba last year.   _____
3   The office was___the second floor.   _____
4   John works____576 67th Street.   _____
5   The students were____this country last year.   _____
6   He is staying____the Washington Hotel.   _____
7   John parks his car ____Second Avenue.   _____
8   Charles has lots of friends ____New York City.   _____
9   He bought his car ____Pennsylvania.   _____
10 The house is ____420 East Boulevard.   _____
11 Were you ____ South America last year?   _____
12 She is working ____Boston now.   _____
13 Is the building ____East Boulevard?   _____
14 No, it's ____the corner of Broadway and Second.   _____
15 Please park the car ____the driveway.   _____

Exercise 102   Use <u>in</u>, <u>on</u>, or <u>at</u>.

Did you learn these expressions?

1   ____the whole, I like this country.   _____
2   He is taking a history course ____present.   _____
3   This course seemed easy ____first.   _____
4   ____ second thought, that is probably true.   _____
5   Charles sits ____back of John.   _____
6   He told us three good jokes ____a row.   _____
7   ____some ways, he is a good teacher.   _____
8   Is he ____work now?   _____
9   We discussed that ____the end of the meeting.   _____
10 ____ any rate, you said the right thing.   _____
11 Did he make that mistake ____purpose?   _____
12 ____the contrary, it wasn't intentional ____all.   _____
13 He doesn't like it. ____fact, he hates it.   _____
14 ____general, the English language is easy.   _____
15 Is that man always ____a hurry?   _____
16 Were you ____home last night?   _____
17 We know ____least fifty new words.   _____
18 Mr. Adams usually arrives ____time.   _____
19 Helen sits right____front of Mary.   _____
20 He's taking English. He's taking French ____addition.   _____

Exercise 103   Complete the questions.

QUESTION	ANSWER
1 What did *you* see?	I saw some pictures.
2 What did he *eat*?	He ate some sandwiches.
3 What —— they ——?	They took that package.
4 What —— you ——?	I brought my new pen.
5 What —— —— ——?	We needed some money.
6 What —— —— ——?	They sent a big box.
7 What —— —— ——?	I made a toy boat for them.
8 What —— —— ——?	We studied English and history.
9 What —— —— ——?	She wore a new dress.
10 What —— —— ——?	He wrote a letter.

Exercise 104   Use that, these, there, or what.

1 *These* photographs are very good.　　　　　　　*These*
2 —— did Mr. Smith say?
3 —— are some books on —— desk.
4 —— did you put in —— boxes?
5 —— were a few new words in —— lesson.
6 —— did you see at —— museum?
7 —— were several people in —— room.
8 —— student is a friend of —— boys.
9 —— is some meat in the refrigerator.
10 —— was ——?

Exercise 105   Use yesterday, last, or ago.

1 She went to the party *last* night.　　　　　*last*
2 They went home about an hour ——.
3 Did you review the lesson —— afternoon?
4 He came to the United States a long time ——.
5 Was Edward in South America —— year?
6 Did he speak to Mr. Smith ——?
7 He taught history here —— semester.
8 We sent the letter over a week ——.
9 We wrote another letter —— morning.
10 Mr. Brown left for Ohio five days ——.
11 They went to the movies —— night.
12 I saw him —— Thursday afternoon.

Exercise 106   Use <u>much</u>, <u>many</u>, or <u>very</u>.

1   There are _many_ chairs in that room.   _many_
2   That brown house is ——— old.   ———
3   The men drink ——— water every day.   ———
4   Charles wasn't ——— thirsty.   ———
5   Does John know ——— English?   ———
6   He works in that ——— large building.   ———
7   Are there ——— students in this class?   ———
8   Does Mr. Brown have ——— money?   ———
9   He usually eats ——— pieces of bread.   ———
10 English is a ——— easy language.   ———

Exercise 107   Use <u>too</u>, <u>too much</u>, or <u>too many</u>.

1   That red house is _too_ big.   _too_
2   There is ——— sugar in the coffee.   ———
3   It is ——— hot today.   ———
4   There were ——— people in the room.   ———
5   The children are making ——— noise.   ———
6   There is ——— water in this glass.   ———
7   These books are ——— difficult for us.   ———
8   There are ——— chairs in that room.   ———
9   We hear ——— advertising on the radio.   ———
10 The Japanese student has ——— friends.   ———

Exercise 108   Use <u>a</u>, <u>an</u>, <u>some</u>, or <u>any</u>.

1   There are _some_ very large buildings here.   _some_
2   There aren't ——— tall buildings in this city.   ———
3   There are ——— sandwiches on the table.   ———
4   There is ——— sandwich on the plate.   ———
5   There weren't ——— chairs in the room.   ———
6   Was there ——— chair in the other room?   ———
7   There are ——— men in the office now.   ———
8   Was there ——— name in the book?   ———
9   There weren't ——— cigarettes in the package.   ———
10 Was there ——— apple on the table?   ———
11 There aren't _any_ plates on the table.   ———
12 Are there _some_ glasses on the table?   ———

79

VOCABULARY FOR LESSON SEVEN

Pages 70 - 79

Adams 73
advertising 79
airmail 74
another 78
ate 70
avenue 71
back 74
beside 74
Bill 73
billfold 75
birthday 76
Boston 71
boulevard 77
bring 70
Broadway 77
brother 76
brought 70
build 70
built 70
choose 70
chose 70
cup 71
destroy 72
did 70
drank 70
driveway 71
drove 70
east 77
Edward 78
eighteen 74
felt 70
fifth 71
find 70
fifty 77
five 74
flew 70
found 70

garage 71
gave 70
gift 76
grew 70
groceries 73
grow 70
hate 72
heard 70
hour 74
intentional 77
introduce 71
irregular 71
Japanese 79
knew 70
lend 76
Long Island 71
love 72
low 74
mail 76
maybe 71
meal 75
mistake 75
museum 74
north 78
Ohio 78
over 78
pair 75
park 78
Pennsylvania 77
piece 79
pocketbook 71
present 76
price 74
probably 77
program 75
prove 71
purse 74

report 71
return 71
review 78
ride 70
rode 70
said 70
sang 70
saw 70
second 77
sent 70
show 76
sidewalk 71
sing 70
skirt 75
slept 70
sold 70
son 76
spent 70
spoke 70
suggest 71
taught 70
tell 70
test 75
throw 76
ticket 76
told 70
took 70
train 75
twelve 74
Venezuela 75
Washington 77
went 70
White 73
wore 70
wrote 70

Yes, Doctor.
English is
very easy.

LESSON EIGHT

8A The irregular verbs (part two)

present	past	present	past
begin	began	lose	lost
bet	bet	make	made
bite	bit	mean	meant
blow	blew	meet	met
break	broke	pay	paid
catch	caught	quit	quit
cost	cost	run	ran
cut	cut	sit	sat
fall	fell	slide	slid
fit	fit	spin	spun
forget	forgot	spread	spread
get	got	stand	stood
have	had	steal	stole
hide	hid	tear	tore
hold	held	think	thought
keep	kept	throw	threw
lead	led	understand	understood
lend	lent	win	won

8B The possessive forms of nouns

BOY'S

That book belongs to
   the boy.

That is the boy's book.

The boy's book is here.

Those books belong to
   the boy.

Those are the boy's books.

The boy's books are here.

BOYS'

That car belongs to
   the two boys.

That is the boys' car.

The boys' car is here.

Those cars belong to
   the two boys.

Those are the boys' cars.

The boys' cars are here.

Study the following examples carefully:

the student's book	John's car	the child's toy
the student's books	John's cars	the child's toys
the students' book	Charles' car	the children's toy
the students' books	Charles' cars	the children's toys

8C   The possessive adjectives

1	my friend, my friends	our friend, our friends
2	your friend, your friends	your friend, your friends
3	his friend, his friends her friend, her friends its friend, its friends	their friends, their friends

Mary's dress	is blue.
Her dress	is blue.

Mary's dresses	are pretty.
Her dresses	are pretty.

That is	John's book.
That is	his book.

Those are	John's books.
Those are	his books.

8D   The possessive pronouns

1	mine	ours
2	yours	yours
3	his hers	theirs

That is	Mary's purse.
That is	hers.

Those are	my books.
Those are	mine.

Their car	is here.
Theirs	is here.

Their cars	are here.
Theirs	are here.

8E   The preposition of

Of indicates possession with objects and things.

The title of the book is short.
The legs of the table are round.
The front of the building is beautiful.

<u>Of</u> occurs in a special possessive expression.

He is a friend of mine.　He's also a friend of Mary's.

<u>Of</u> indicates quality or quantity.

Jack is a boy of sixteen.　　　　a cup of coffee
Jack is sixteen years of age.　　a glass of milk
(Jack is sixteen years old.)　　a piece of bread
She is a woman of great beauty.　a pair of shoes
(She is a very beautiful woman.)　a crowd of people

<u>Of</u> indicates apposition.

The City of Detroit　　　The University of California
The City of Miami　　　The University of Detroit
The State of Louisiana　but: Yale University
but:　The City of New York　　Columbia University
or:　New York City　　　Michigan State University
　　　　　　　　　　　　　Washington Square College

8F　Idioms

<u>beg one's pardon:</u>　I beg your pardon.　-- That's all right.
<u>Beg your pardon.</u>　I didn't see you.　-- Quite all right.

<u>change one's mind:</u>　Did you change your mind about that?
I often change my mind about things.　He changed his mind.

<u>do one's best:</u>　I always do my best in class.　Did you do
your best on the examination?　-- Yes, I did my best on it.

<u>get rid of:</u>　He bought a new car.　-- Did he get rid of his
old car first?　Did he get rid of that cold of his last week?

<u>in one's opinion:</u>　In my opinion, that is the right answer.

<u>in spite of:</u>　I went to the movies in spite of the bad weather.

<u>lose one's temper:</u>　He was very mad.　In fact, he lost his
temper.　-- Did you lose your temper during the argument?

<u>of course:</u>　Of course, some people don't agree with that.
Of course you're right.　Of course, it was not very easy.

<u>take a course in:</u>　Did he take a course in English last year?

<u>take advantage of:</u>　Did they take advantage of your offer?

<u>take an examination</u> (or <u>test</u>): Did you take an examination?

EXERCISES FOR LESSON EIGHT

Exercise 109 Write the past tense form of the verb for each sentence.

(part one)

1 The wind (blow) hard. _____ *The wind blew hard.*
2 He (forget) the name of it. _____
3 The boys (run) down the street. _____
4 She (throw) it into the wastebasket. _____
5 The party (begin) at eight o'clock. _____
6 I (sit) in the seat behind Tom. _____
7 You (make) several mistakes on the test. _____
8 The man (hide) the money in the drawer. _____
9 The girl (break) her pocket mirror. _____
10 We (pay) a lot of bills last month. _____
11 They (lend) us nine dollars yesterday. _____
12 The thief (steal) all of the money. _____
13 The police (catch) him a short time later. _____
14 I (stand) on the corner for an hour. _____
15 She (meet) the new student yesterday. _____

(part two)

16 The boy (hold) the box very carefully. _____
17 Tom and Bill (have) dinner with us. _____
18 We (bet) two dollars on the election. _____
19 I (fall) on the front steps of the house. _____
20 She (tear) her dress on the sharp corner. _____
21 The dog (bite) the mailman yesterday. _____
22 Mr. Williams (quit) his job last week. _____
23 Our team (win) the game yesterday. _____
24 However, the team (lose) its previous game. _____
25 His new suit (cost) eighty-five dollars. _____
26 The suit (fit) him very well. _____
27 He (get) the suit at that store. _____
28 I (cut) my hand with a razor blade. _____
29 She (keep) the money in her purse. _____
30 Mr. and Mrs. Brown (buy) that house. _____
31 She (lose) her purse last night. _____
32 I (spread) the butter on the bread. _____
33 The wheels of the car (spin) very fast. _____

Exercise 110 Change these statements to questions.

(part one)

1 Robert was here. _____ *Was Robert here?*
2 His father works for a big company. _____
3 I went to school with him in New York. _____
4 There were some interesting people there. _____
5 His friend finished the work for him. _____
6 He is a very good friend of mine. _____
7 Alice drove her car downtown. _____
8 She is Mr. Brown's daughter. _____
9 Charles always learns the new words. _____
10 He forgot the meaning of that word. _____
11 There was a meeting here last night. _____
12 Mr. Williams knows Charles very well. _____
13 I lost my new ballpoint pen yesterday. _____
14 The women were in the kitchen. _____
15 He walked downtown with John and Tom. _____

(part two)

16 Betty cooked the dinner last night. _____
17 We were ready at two o'clock. _____
18 Mary's mother made that dress by hand. _____
19 Mr. Adams teaches English. _____
20 They are Charles' brothers. _____
21 We saw them the night before last. _____
22 There is an empty bottle on the shelf. _____
23 This briefcase belongs to Mr. Smith. _____
24 She is picking up the papers now. _____
25 My friend lent me five dollars. _____
26 Tom owes me four dollars. _____
27 I took the papers out of my briefcase. _____
28 There are lots of sandwiches on the plate. _____
29 They came at 4:30 p.m. yesterday. _____
30 That tall boy is a friend of his. _____
31 Charles cut his hand' with a razor blade. _____
32 He usually leaves his car here. _____
33 I put the money in that drawer. _____
34 His new suit fits him very well. _____
35 It cost eighty-five dollars. _____

Exercise 111   Change these statements to negatives.

(part one)

1   He changed his mind. _____*He didn't change his mind.*
2   She's a relative of mine. _____
3   Tom's father gave him the money. _____
4   There were a lot of people at the party. _____
5   She kept up with all of the homework. _____
6   It was quite hot yesterday. _____
7   Tom lost his temper during the argument. _____
8   There were some cigarettes on the table. _____
9   I am looking forward to that test. _____
10   Tom is never at home at this hour. _____
11   He drives quite carefully. _____
12   They got rid of their house. _____
13   There are lots of lessons in this book. _____
14   John seldom comes to class on time. _____
15   She does the dishes every day. _____

(part two)

16   I am studying history this semester. _____
17   They took advantage of his offer. _____
18   There were a lot of new words in that lesson. _____
19   These sentences are quite difficult. _____
20   John took care of the garden during our vacation. _____
21   I hear the airplane. _____
22   She learned all of the words by heart. _____
23   Miss Brown never studies very hard. _____
24   I do my lessons on the bus. _____
25   We sent the letter to them by airmail. _____
26   There were some big boxes on the floor. _____
27   The boys made fun of Bob's old car. _____
28   It was quite cold the day before last. _____
29   Mary did the work carefully. _____
30   She had some trouble with it. _____
31   I did my best on that test. _____
32   He lost his temper in spite of that. _____
33   The news spread very quickly. _____
34   She wore her new summer dress. _____
35   She changed her mind about the trip. _____

Exercise 112 Change the title to "Yesterday." Change all of the verbs to the past tense.

EVER Y DAY

got up   *took*
I get up at 7:30 a.m.   Then I take a shower.   Afterwards I put on my clothes and go to breakfast.   I eat cereal, toast, and eggs.   I drink a glass of milk too.   Then I study for half an hour.   I leave the house at 8:45 and meet my friend at the corner.   We walk to school together and talk about different things.   We arrive there at 8:58.   We run to the classroom quickly and wait for the teacher.   All of the students laugh and tell jokes until nine o'clock.   The teacher comes at nine and shuts the door.   Then the students become very quiet.

First the teacher asks questions about the assignment. Later he talks about the new lesson and teaches the students new words.   They listen to him carefully.   Then they practice the new words.   At the end of the hour, he gives the assignment for the next day.

I attend my other classes between ten o'clock and noon. I have my lunch at the cafeteria with John. We work at the library in the afternoon.   I return home at 4:40.   Then I take care of many little things around the house.   After dinner, I watch television for an hour.   Then I spend two hours on my lessons for the next day.

Exercise 113 Write the correct possessive form of each underlined word.

1	(Mary) sister is pretty.	*Mary's*
2	I took that (girl) pencil by mistake.	_____
3	Are the (boys) coats in the closet?	_____
4	Mrs. (Brown) new dress is cute.	_____
5	The (men) work was very good.	_____
6	That brown house is Mr. (Smith).	_____
7	The (students) papers are on the desk.	_____
8	The yellow book is (John).	_____
9	Are the (children) toys on the floor?	_____
10	Is (Tom) friend in the other class?	_____
11	Mr. (Williams) son studied at that college.	_____
12	The (doctor) office is on the ninth floor.	_____
13	The two (lawyers) office is on the same floor.	_____
14	Do you know that (man) name?	_____
15	(Edward) English isn't very good.	_____
16	Is that old brown car (Bob)?	_____
17	The three (girls) apartment is nice.	_____
18	The (teacher) desk is near the door.	_____
19	Betty is (Martha) niece.	_____
20	(Betty) brother is (Martha) nephew.	_____
	Martha is their _____.	

Exercise 114 Write the possessive adjective form of the underlined word in each sentence.

1	The boy is writing with _his_ pen.	*his*
2	The girl is reading _her_ letters now.	*her*
3	John and Charles eat with _____ friend.	_____
4	Mr. Brown usually drives _____ car to work.	_____
5	Mary is using _____ sister's book.	_____
6	I studied _____ lesson carefully last night.	_____
7	The students brought _____ papers to class.	_____
8	_____ full name is John Peter Smith.	_____
9	We ate _____ lunch at 11:30.	_____
10	I always bring _____ books to class.	_____
11	John and _____ brother are studying French.	_____
12	The children left _____ toys on the floor.	_____
13	The man put _____ coat in the closet.	_____
14	We visited _____ aunt in Chicago last summer.	_____
15	What did you write on _____ paper?	_____

Exercise 115   Write <u>her</u> or <u>hers</u> in each blank space.

1 _____purse is on the table.   her, hers
2 _____ is on the table now.   her, hers
3 Does she have _____book?   her, hers
4 Does she have _____?   her, hers
5 These are _____ exercises.   her, hers
6 Those are _____ too.   her, hers
7 Is this_____?   her, hers
8 Are these _____?   her, hers
9 Is this _____ pencil?   her, hers
10 Are these _____ pencils?   her, hers

Exercise 116   Write <u>their</u> or <u>theirs</u> in each blank space.

1 Are _____coats in the closet?   their, theirs
2 _____ books are in this room.   their, theirs
3 Is _____ house very large?   their, theirs
4 Is this_____?   their, theirs
5 Are these _____ ?   their, theirs
6 Those are _____ exercises.   their, theirs
7 Does _____ friend like it here?   their, theirs
8 Do they have _____pencils?   their, theirs
9 _____car is over there.   their, theirs
10 _____ is the red one.   their, theirs

Exercise 117   Substitute possessive pronouns for the underlined words.

1 That is <u>my book</u>. _____ *That is mine.*
2 Those are <u>his cigarettes</u>. _____
3 Is that <u>your book</u> or <u>her book</u>? _____
4 That house is <u>the Browns' house</u>. _____
5 Are these my pencils or <u>the girl's pencils</u>? _____
6 That car is <u>my brother's car</u>. _____
7 Is that newspaper <u>your newspaper</u>? _____
8 Those notebooks are <u>their notebooks</u>. _____
9 He took her pen and left <u>my pen</u>. _____
10 Are these papers <u>his papers</u>? _____
11 Frank lent me <u>his sister's book</u>. _____
12 He gave me <u>his matches</u>. _____
13 That car is <u>my friend's car</u>. _____
14 These magazines are <u>their magazines</u>. _____
15 Those are <u>Miss Brown's cigarettes</u>. _____

Exercise 118 Add <u>a</u> or <u>an</u> if necessary.

1 She is   very pretty girl. _____
2 Mr. Brown bought   new car last week. _____
3 Edward is   good student. _____
4 Those boys are   good students. _____
5 Our lesson lasts for   hour and   half. _____
6 Tom always eats   egg for breakfast. _____
7 They are   doctors from Europe. _____
8 That is   very expensive car. _____
9 I have   afternoon classes. _____
10 There are   chairs in that room. _____
11 Bill is   American citizen. _____
12 Do you have   food in your kitchen? _____
13 They sell   furniture in that store. _____
14 We sent   letter to John last Tuesday. _____
15 There are   sandwiches on the table. _____

Exercise 119 Use only the <u>simple present tense</u> or the <u>continuous present tense</u> of the indicated verb.

1 He (speak) to John now. _He's speaking to John now._
2 Listen! Someone (knock) at the door. _____
3 He often (leave) town on business. _____
4 The drugstore (have) a sale today. _____
5 I never (go) there in the afternoon. _____
6 At present, he (write) a history book. _____
7 She (go) to bed at ten during the week. _____
8 John (seem) very busy right now. _____
9 That student (study) every evening. _____
10 This class (meet) from 8:30 to 9:45 p.m. _____
11 I (hear) a noise right now! _____
12 The man (use) the telephone now. _____
13 Yes, I (see) the airplane now. _____
14 It (rain) very much in the spring. _____
15 Bill (sit) at the other desk today. _____
16 We (need) some money right away. _____
17 They (listen) to the radio right now. _____
18 We (learn) the irregular verbs this week. _____
19 Yes, he (want) some coffee. _____
20 She (take) some medicine for her cold. _____

90

Exercise 120 Use the correct tense of the verb in each sentence.

(part one)

1   She (work) right now. _____ *She is working right now.*
2   He (like) cigars. _____ *He likes cigars.*
3   I (walk) in the park yesterday. _____
4   Frank usually (know) the answers. _____
5   The boys (go) to the football game yesterday. _____
6   John (drink) a lot of coffee every day. _____
7   Mr. Brown (buy) a new overcoat last fall. _____
8   The girls always (study) the lesson at night. _____
9   She (give) the book to me last night. _____
10 We (open) the door an hour ago. _____
11 They (be) at the concert last night. _____
12 Miss Brown (shop) at the store right now. _____
13 There (be) many people here yesterday. _____
14 Some students always (come) to class on time. _____
15 I (read) that article in the paper last night. _____

(part two)

16 Mary (be) sick yesterday. _____
17 Mr. Smith (sell) his house last year. _____
18 She (wash) the dishes right now. _____
19 The men (listen) to the radio last night. _____
20 The Browns (fly) to Europe every summer. _____
21 The company (build) an apartment house there now._
22 Betty (choose) a pretty dress at the store yesterday.
23 At present, she (wear) a skirt and blouse. _____
24 It (snow) very much every winter. _____
25 The man (leave) for Chicago an hour ago. _____
26 My friend (speak) to him right now. _____
27 Tom and I (ride) with him yesterday morning. _____
28 Listen! I (hear) an airplane. _____
29 Betty (wear) a red and white dress last night. _____
30 Listen! Someone (call) your name. _____
31 They (break) the window several days ago. _____
32 The wind (blow) very hard last night. _____
33 She always (forget) my name. _____
34 They (take) the examination right now. _____
35 Charles (offer) him some money last week. _____

VOCABULARY FOR LESSON EIGHT

Pages 81 - 91

argument 86
around 87
article 91
become 87
began 81
bet 81
between 87
bit 81
bite 81
blew 81
blow 81
break 81
briefcase 85
broke 81
business 90
careful 85
catch 81
caught 81
cereal 87
Chicago 88
citizen 90
college 83
cook 85
cost 81
crowd 83
cut 81
daughter 85
Detroit 83
different 87
down 84
dozen 83
drugstore 90
eighty 84
election 84
evening 90
father 85
fell 81
first 87
fit 81
forget 81

forgot 81
got 81
had 81
half 87
held 81
hers 82
hid 81
hide 81
homework 86
its 82
job 84
kept 81
later 84
lead 81
led 81
leg 82
lent 81
lose 81
lost 81
Louisiana 83
mad 83
made 81
mailman 84
meaning 85
meet 81
met 81
Michigan 83
mine 82
my 82
nephew 87
niece 87
nine 84
noon 87
offer 83
our 82
ours 82
paid 81
pocket 84
previous 84
quiet 87

quit 81
ran 81
razor blade 84
relative 86
round 82
run 81
sat 81
seat 84
sister 90
sixteen 83
slid 81
slide 81
spin 81
spread 81
spun 81
stand 81
state 83
steal 81
steps 84
stole 81
stood 81
team 84
tear 81
their 82
theirs 82
then 87
threw 82
title 82
together 87
tore 81
trouble 86
understood 81
until 87
wait 87
wheel 84
win 81
wind 84
won 81
your 82
yours 82

92

LESSON NINE

9A   Summary of the possessive forms

subject	object	possessive forms	
I	me	mine	<u>my</u> book, <u>my</u> books
you	you	yours	<u>your</u> book, <u>your</u> books
he	him	his	<u>his</u> book, <u>his</u> books
she	her	hers	<u>her</u> book, <u>her</u> books
it	it		<u>its</u> eye, <u>its</u> eyes

subject	object	possessive forms	
we	us	ours	<u>our</u> book, <u>our</u> books
you	you	yours	<u>your</u> book, <u>your</u> books
they	them	theirs	<u>their</u> book, <u>their</u> books

9B   The future tense with *will*

The word <u>will</u> expresses the future time. <u>Will</u> does not
change in form. (Some speakers use the forms <u>I shall</u>
and <u>we shall</u>. However, the forms <u>I will</u> or <u>I'll</u> and <u>we
will</u> or <u>we'll</u> are current and generally easier for non-
native speakers of English.)

Present:	He		works	very hard every day.
Past:	He		worked	very hard yesterday.
Future:	He	will	work	very hard tomorrow.

Examples:

I am ready now.	I will be ready in one hour.
He is here now.	He will be here tomorrow.
She comes every day.	She will come tomorrow.
We ate there yesterday.	We will eat there next week.

9C Statements, questions, and negatives

	They	will			be	here	tomorrow.
Will	they				be	here	tomorrow?
	They	will	not		be	here	tomorrow.

	They	will		go	there	tomorrow.
Will	they			go	there	tomorrow?
	They	will	not	go	there	tomorrow.

9D Contractions with *will*

I will	=	I'll
you will	=	you'll
he will	=	he'll

etc.

I will not	=	I won't
you will not	=	you won't
they will not	=	they won't

etc.

9E *In, on,* and *at* in expressions of time (part one)

IN	ON	AT
June 1954 the winter the spring the summer the fall the morning the afternoon the evening the past the future	June tenth Tuesday Tuesday morning Tuesday afternoon Tuesday evening Tuesday night	noon noon yesterday noon tomorrow night two o'clock midnight
	In these examples, the preposition <u>on</u> is optional. <u>On</u> is frequently omitted before the expressions <u>Tuesday morning</u>, <u>Tuesday afternoon</u>, etc.	

9F Idioms

<u>at a time</u>: He went down the steps two at a time.

<u>at last</u>: At last, they found the answer to the question.

94

at one time: (1) Both of the students spoke at one time. (2) At one time, he had a lot of money. I knew it at one time.

at that time: Frank and Tom were in the navy at that time.

at the same time: Both of the boys spoke at the same time.

at times: At times, she enjoys a good historical novel.

in case of: In case of rain, the people will stay at home.

in no time: He returned with the money in no time. In no time at all, they finished the work. I did it in no time.

in succession: Charles wrote three letters in succession.

in that case: In that case, the men will be very careful.

in the beginning: In the beginning, they didn't understand English very well. That was quite easy in the beginning.

in the end: In the end, the two policemen caught the thief.

in the event of: In the event of a fire, call the fire department right away. Call us by phone in the event of trouble.

in the first place: I don't like that man. In the first place, he's too impolite. In the second place, he talks too much.

in the long run: In the long run, the English language will be very important to you. I prefer this one in the long run.

in the meantime: We went to the store. In the meantime, they prepared the dinner. In the meantime, she waited.

in the nick of time: He jumped in the nick of time. The car missed him by inches. He did it just in the nick of time.

in time for: I came in time for the second half of the movie.

on occasion: On occasion, I enjoy a good television program.

on the spur of the moment: We decided on the spur of the moment. On the spur of the moment, he decided to leave.

on time: Mr. Brown almost always gets to work on time.

EXERCISES FOR LESSON NINE

Exercise 121   Use the future tense of the indicated verb in each sentence.

1   We (meet) you tomorrow. *We will meet you tomorrow.*
2   The party (begin) at nine o'clock. _____
3   I (give) him the money tomorrow. _____
4   We (have) an important holiday next month. _____
5   Mr. Smith (lock) the door afterwards. _____
6   She (remind) him of that. _____
7   We (be) ready at one o'clock. _____
8   His wife (buy) the fruit and vegetables. _____
9   The professor (read) the poem to us. _____
10 Tom (collect) the tickets at the door. _____
11 The men (be) here at 2:30 sharp. _____
12 They (wait) for us on the corner. _____
13 They (translate) the book into English. _____
14 You (ruin) your new clothes. _____
15 I (explain) this custom to you. _____

Exercise 122   Change the verb in each sentence to the future tense.

1   I ate a steak for dinner. *I will eat a steak for dinner.*
2   John spoke to the Dutch girl. _____
3   My friend lent me some money. _____
4   He went to the opera with Charles. _____
5   Mr. Williams got to his office on time. _____
6   The Browns flew to Argentina. _____
7   The man wore his new topcoat. _____
8   The clerk gave Charles the change. _____
9   We heard an interesting lecture. _____
10 I brought the application blank. _____
11 Our guests saw almost all of the city. _____
12 Edward wrote a description of his city. _____
13 They read the article in the magazine. _____
14 She bought a new pair of high-heel shoes. _____
15 The professor said some interesting things. _____
16 You made a lot of mistakes on the paper. _____
17 Tom sold his old car to a friend of his. _____
18 He put the packages on the table. _____

Exercise 123   Change these statements to questions.

1   He will attend our class. ___*Will he attend our class?*___
2   They will be there at noon. _____
3   They will arrive late tomorrow. _____
4   Mary will be late for the meeting. _____
5   I will leave the airport at six. _____
6   John will finish his work before noon. _____
7   Mr. Smith will be back in a few minutes. _____
8   This exercise will seem very easy to you. _____
9   There will be a list of names here. _____
10 The teacher will speak to them this afternoon. _____
11 The girls will be in Dallas, Texas, by tomorrow. _____
12 She will see John tomorrow night. _____
13 John will call for her at 8:00 p.m. _____
14 He will speak to her in English all evening. _____
15 They will go to the late movie. _____

Exercise 124   Change these statements to negatives.

1   He will travel by air. ___*He will not travel by air.*___
2   John will be at home tonight. _____
3   The letter will arrive in the morning. _____
4   The men will be here before four. _____
5   We will meet them at the airport. _____
6   It will be quite hot tomorrow. _____
7   We will send the letter by special delivery. _____
8   They will stay at that hotel tonight. _____
9   There will be quite a few people there. _____
10 They will get back before six-thirty. _____
11 The papers will be on my desk tomorrow. _____
12 Tom will bring a lot of guests to the party. _____
13 You will remember his name. _____
14 This will be very easy for you. _____
15 He will tell you some of the answers. _____
16 They will leave from Grand Central Station. _____
17 There will be some new students in the class. _____
18 I will be quite busy tomorrow afternoon. _____
19 We will take a boat from Miami to Havana. _____
20 The box will weigh quite a bit. _____
21 The Browns will be at the meeting. _____
22 The plane will leave before midnight. _____

97

Exercise 125 Use <u>in</u>, <u>on</u>, or <u>at</u> with each expression of time. Use the expressions with this sentence:

He saw his friend_____

1 ___Monday
2 ___night
3 ___July 4
4 ___the winter
5 ___4:30 p.m.

6 ___noon
7 ___1949
8 ___midnight
9 ___the evening
10 ___Oct. 20, 1950

11 ___3:30 p.m.
12 ___Saturday
13 ___the morning
14 ___April third
15 ___the spring

Exercise 126 Use <u>in</u>, <u>on</u>, or <u>at</u> with each expression of time. Use the expressions with this sentence:

He will see his friend_____

1 ___the evening
2 ___midnight
3 ___1969
4 ___May 13
5 ___noon

6 ___9:45 a.m.
7 ___the afternoon
8 ___Friday
9 ___eight-fifteen
10 ___Sunday night

11 ___night
12 ___August
13 ___August 21
14 ___seven
15 ___the summer

Exercise 127 Make contractions if possible.

1 I will open the door.
2 He will not be there
3 They will be there.
4 I will not be there.
5 You will be tired.
6 We will not be ready.
7 It will not be easy.
8 She will do it.
9 We will see him.
10 They will not be here.
11 It will be ready.
12 He will write to them.
13 They will not see it.
14 I will talk to him.
15 She will not come.
16 They will not be here.
17 It will not be easy.
18 We will be ready.
19 She will not be late.
20 I will send it soon.

Exercise 128 Make contractions if possible.

1 She is not a teacher.
2 John does not like it.
3 I am not very tired.
4 They were not there.
5 I will leave very soon.
6 It did not rain at all.
7 She does not know it.
8 It is a pretty house.
9 There are not any here.
10 We will not see him.
11 They were not ready.
12 She will answer him.
13 I do not know him.
14 John was not late.
15 He is the new teacher.
16 We did not see them.
17 I will not be at home.
18 I am not a club member.
19 What is a "club?"
20 That is an organization.

98

Exercise 129   Use <u>in</u>, <u>on</u>, or <u>at</u> in each sentence.

1 They will leave late ____ the afternoon.   ____
2 Frank arrived ____ New York ____ noon.   ____
3 ____ second thought, you are probably right.   ____
4 The weather is usually warm ____ August.   ____
5 The weather is pleasant ____ the spring.   ____
6 ____ times, he says some really funny things.   ____
7 The mailman delivered the letter ____ 1:45 p.m.   ____
8 They will finish the work ____ no time ____ all.   ____
9 Did you get to the meeting ____ time yesterday?   ____
10 He woke up ____ two o'clock ____ the morning.   ____
11 Mary answered two questions ____ succession.   ____
12 The Browns live ____ Eighth Avenue.   ____
13 ____ occasion, they see a play ____ Broadway.   ____
14 Her brother's birthday is ____ March 13.   ____
15 ____ the first place, I really don't enjoy it.   ____
16 I often do things ____ the spur of the moment.   ____
17 ____ general, does he do good work ____ class?   ____
18 No, ____ the contrary, he doesn't try hard ____ all. ____
19 They arrived home ____ June 10 ____ midnight.   ____
20 ____ the meantime, he wrote it ____ the blackboard. ____
21 Yes, I closed the door ____ purpose.   ____
22 I saw him ____ Chicago ____ June, 1945.   ____
23 ____ present, he is writing another book.   ____
24 Did they buy their car ____ Los Angeles or here?   ____
25 We will see them ____ the third of February.   ____
26 ____ the end, we decided against it.   ____
27 This book seemed quite easy ____ first.   ____
28 They were ____ Greece and Italy ____ 1952.   ____
29 He will bring along ____ least two friends.   ____
30 The garage is ____ back of the house.   ____
31 ____ the whole, our vacation ____ Europe was pleasant.
32 Mr. Wilson works ____ 667 76th Street ____ New York.
33 Both of the men spoke ____ the same time.   ____
34 He is staying ____ the Lincoln Hotel ____ Boston. ____
35 This will probably come true ____ the future.   ____
36 ____ the past, that was almost always true.   ____
37 He spoke about it ____ several different occasions. ____
38 ____ some parts of the country, they do that.   ____
39 Did you mail the letter ____ the fifteenth of the month?
40 You made two mistakes ____ that sentence.   ____

Exercise 130 Show possession with of, 's, or s' .

1 I knew (man - address). ___*I knew the man's address.*
2 He knew (book - name). *He knew the name of the book.*
3 (house - roof) is very high. _____
4 (front - building) is beautiful. _____
5 (coats - girls) are there. _____
6 We borrowed (boys - car). _____
7 Tom is (friend - hers). _____
8 Those are (student - notebooks). _____
9 Those are (students - notebooks). _____
10 (cover - book) is good-looking. _____
11 (top - desk) was quite dirty. _____
12 (car - John) is in (garage - Mr. Smith). _____
13 (camera - price) is very low. _____
14 Helen is (Tom - sister). _____
15 She is a (mine - relative). _____

Exercise 131 Substitute is or are for belong(s) to.
Change the following word to the possessive form.

1 That purse belongs to her. _____*That purse is hers.*
2 This car belongs to Bob. _____*This car is his.*
3 That notebook belongs to him. _____
4 The gray sweater belongs to me. _____
5 The white house belongs to them. _____
6 This briefcase belongs to Mr. Smith. _____
7 The pencils belong to you. _____
8 That old furniture belongs to me. _____
9 These overshoes belong to Mr. Adams. _____
10 These leather notebooks belong to her. _____

Exercise 132 Rewrite these sentences. Use the pattern
given in the two examples.

1 That jacket belongs to her. _____*That is her jacket.*
2 This notebook belongs to me. ___*This is my notebook.*
3 That house belongs to them. _____
4 This land belongs to Mr. Smith. _____
5 This money belongs to you. _____
6 That television set belongs to Brown. _____
7 These watches belong to him. _____
8 That umbrella belongs to Betty. _____
9 Those shoes don't belong to me. _____
10 This billfold doesn't belong to her. _____

100

Exercise 133 Use <u>was</u>, <u>were</u>, or <u>did</u> in each sentence.

1 ____ the lecture interesting? _____
2 What ____ he speak about? _____
3 What ____ the title of the lecture? _____
4 ____ you hear all of it? _____
5 ____ there many people there? _____
6 ____ you there before 8:00 p.m.? _____
7 ____ there a question period? _____
8 ____ you ask any questions? _____
9 What ____ he say? _____
10 What ____ the answer? _____

Exercise 134 Select the correct verb for each sentence.
Use the past tense. Use each verb only one time.

take
lose
fall
✓go
choose
tear
grow
spend
break
throw
hurt
forget

1 The boy *went* home an hour ago. *went*
2 John ____ the boy's last name. _____
3 The tree ____ a lot last year. _____
4 He ____ the ball over the wall. _____
5 I ____ a pretty tie at the store. _____
6 She ____ her dress on a sharp nail. _____
7 They ____ a French course last year. _____
8 We ____ all of our money yesterday. _____
9 The boy ____ the glass window. _____
10 I ____ on the ice and ____ my arm. _____
11 She ____ her purse at school. _____

Exercise 135 Use <u>yesterday</u>, <u>last</u>, or <u>ago</u>.

1 We went to a party ____ night. _____
2 They planned the party a week ____. _____
3 They had a meeting ____ Friday. _____
4 They bought the coffee several days ____. _____
5 They made the sandwiches ____ afternoon. _____
6 They invited Mr. Smith ____ week. _____
7 They sent the invitations five days ____. _____
8 The boys made the decorations ____ Wednesday. _____
9 The boys decorated the room ____ morning. _____
10 There were many people there ____ night. _____
11 They left only a few hours ____. _____
12 We knew about it early ____ week. _____

101

VOCABULARY FOR LESSON NINE

Pages 93 - 101

action 95
against 99
air 97
airport 97
almost 96
application 96
April 98
Argentina 96
blank 96
both 94
change 96
club 98
collect 96
custom 96
Dallas 97
decide 95
decorate 101
decoration 101
deliver 99
description 96
Dutch 96
February 99
fire department 95
fire extinguisher 95
Friday 98
gray 100
Greece 99
Havana 97
high heel shoes 96
historical 94
holiday 96
hometown 96
impolite 95
inch 95
invitation 101
Johnson 96
jump 95

land 100
leather 100
list 97
lock 96
Los Angeles 99
March 99
member 98
midnight 94
nail 101
navy 94
novel 94
opera 96
organization 98
period 101
plan 101
pleasant 99
poem 96
professor 96
really 99
remind 96
ruin 96
set 100
seventh 98
sharp 96
something 99
special delivery 97
stay 97
steak 96
tenth 94
Texas 97
thief 95
third 98
tomorrow 93
tonight 93
top 100
topcoat 96
translate 96

vegetable 96
wife 96
wonderful 99
won't 94

English is easy.

LESSON TEN

10A Expressions of time (part two)

These expressions do not require a preposition.

PAST	FUTURE
yesterday yesterday morning yesterday afternoon	tomorrow tomorrow morning tomorrow afternoon
last evening last night	tomorrow evening tomorrow night
last Thursday last Thursday morning, etc. last week, month, year last June, June tenth	next Tuesday next Tuesday morning, etc. next week, month, year next June, June tenth

PAST, PRESENT, or FUTURE

today, tonight, this morning, this afternoon, this week, etc.

10B Expressions of time (part three)

These expressions do not require a preposition.

a minute ago several hours ago a day ago two days ago a week ago a week ago today a week ago yesterday a week ago last Thursday	a minute from now several hours from now a day from now two days from now a week from now a week from today a week from tomorrow a week from next Tuesday
the day before last the day before yesterday	the day after next the day after tomorrow
the week before last the month before last the year before last	the week after next the month after next the year after next

10C Future substitutes: *be + going to*

I am going to study	we are going to study
you are going to study	you are going to study
he / she is going to study	they are going to study

Examples:

We are going to see that movie tomorrow.
He is going to go to California next month.
I am going to leave in a little while.
They are going to come here again next year.

10D Future substitutes: the present tenses

The present tenses sometimes express future action.   In these cases, a time word (<u>tomorrow</u>, etc.) is usually included in the sentence.

The common verbs in this type of expression are: <u>arrive</u>, <u>come</u>, <u>depart</u>, <u>go</u>, <u>leave</u>, <u>return</u>.

	They	are going	to leave	for Miami tomorrow.
or	They	are leaving		for Miami tomorrow.
or	They	leave		for Miami tomorrow.

10E Short answers

QUESTION	SHORT ANSWER
Are the Smiths ready yet?	Yes, they are.
Was Charles at the meeting?	No, he wasn't.
Were there any people outside?	Yes, there were.
Does Mary like it now?	Yes, she does.
Did the boys go to the party?	No, they didn't.
Will you be here tomorrow?	No, I won't.
Will you give the book to him?	Yes, I will.
Will there be enough coffee?	No, there won't.
Are the men going to do it?	Yes, they are.
Is Mr. Smith leaving tomorrow?	No, he isn't.

No contraction is possible with short answers of this type:
<u>Yes, they are.</u>   <u>Yes, I will.</u>   <u>Yes, she is.</u>   <u>Yes, I am.</u>

104

10F   The prepositions *in, for, by,* and *until*

__I N__   (__at the end of a period of -- __)

>   We will return in ten minutes.
>   or: We will return ten minutes from now.
>   They will be here in half an hour.
>   or: They will be here half an hour from now.
>   He will be back in a little while.

__F O R__   (__within the time limits of -- __)

>   We were in Europe (for) two months.
>   He will be in Venezuela (for) a year.
>   [__For__ is optional in the preceding examples.]
>   They won't be here for half an hour yet.
>   The two men won't be back for a while.

__B Y__   (__before__ --, __not later than__ --)

>   They will be here by noon tomorrow.
>   He will finish the work by two o'clock.

__U N T I L__   (__up to the time__ --)

>   We waited for him until four o'clock.
>   They will work until noon tomorrow.
>   He will be there from June until August.
>   or: He will be there from June to August.

10G   Idioms

__forever__ [usually written as one word in the United States]:
Are those people going to stay in France forever?

__for good__ [an informal substitute for __forever__]:   They have
gone to California for good.   I'm here for good now.

__for long__ [a short form of __for a long time__ occurring only in
sentences with negative words]:   He didn't stay for long.

__for once__: For once, the students didn't make any mistakes.

__for the first time__: You have said the word correctly for
the first time.   For the first time in his life, he agreed.

__from now on__: Please be much more careful from now on.

__from time to time__: We see the Wilsons from time to time.

EXERCISES FOR LESSON TEN

Exercise 136   Use the future with <u>going to</u>.

(part one)

1   I will see it tomorrow. _I am going to see it tomorrow._
2   George will be at home tonight. _____
3   We will finish our homework tomorrow. _____
4   She will arrive in Detroit next week. _____
5   His parents will return at midnight. _____

6   Will they go by plane? _____
7   Will many people attend the meeting? _____
8   Will he assist you with the work? _____
9   Will there be a conference next month? _____
10 Will you finish the work for him? _____

11 I won't leave early. _____
12 There won't be enough sandwiches. _____
13 They won't be ready on time. _____
14 We won't pay any attention to that. _____
15 I won't visit my grandparents this year. _____

(part two)

16 John will write us a letter next week. _____
17 He won't have any time before then. _____
18 Will dinner be ready soon? _____
19 There will be a concert in the park. _____
20 Will the club have a contest? _____
21 They will divide the members into two groups. _____
22 They won't give a prize until later. _____
23 Will you take pictures during your vacation? _____
24 We won't take a camera with us. _____
25 I will meet my cousin in Denver. _____
26 Will you leave on the night train? _____
27 We won't travel by train this time. _____
28 She will speak to Mr. Smith at school. _____
29 We won't clean the house until Friday. _____
30 Will there be enough food for everyone? _____
31 There will be a lot of people at the meeting. _____
32 We will need a lot of coffee and sandwiches. _____
33 The people won't leave here until later. _____
34 Will they return after the meeting? _____

106

Exercise 137 Change these sentences to the future time. Write each sentence in the three indicated ways.

1	They went by train.	*They will go by train.* *They are going to go by train.* *They are going by train.*

2 He arrived at Grand Central Station. _____
3 George left his home at nine o'clock. _____
4 He came to New York on the 5:30 train. _____
5 She departed for Washington by plane. _____
6 We arrived in Paris in the spring. _____
7 They left the city with their friend. _____
8 He came into the city at two-thirty. _____
9 She went to the movies with them. _____
10 I arrived late in the afternoon. _____

Exercise 138 Change these sentences to the future time. Write each sentence in the two indicated ways.

1	I listened to it.	*I will listen to it.* *I am going to listen to it.*

2 She saw them in the morning. _____
3 They bought a new house there. _____
4 Did you watch that television program? _____
5 They sold their car to Mr. Brown. _____
6 He chose several new neckties. _____
7 She wore her best dress to the party. _____
8 He quit his job on Wednesday. _____
9 They spent all of their money there. _____
10 The child is eating his lunch. _____
11 The boys were late for the movie. _____
12 They had some difficulty with it. _____
13 The teacher gave us an example. _____
14 Did they accept his offer? _____
15 No, they didn't accept it. _____
16 Did the students read that book? _____
17 The dinner wasn't ready until 7:30 p.m. _____
18 There were not any speakers at the meeting. _____
19 There wasn't enough time for that. _____
20 Charles stayed at home all day. _____
21 They finished the work before noon. _____
22 He paid his bills with the money. _____

Exercise 139 Change these statements with irrelgular verbs to questions with <u>be</u> + <u>going</u> and the indicated time expression.

(part one)

1 They took it yesterday. (tomorrow)_____
   Are you going to take it tomorrow?
2 She brought it last night. (tomorrow night)_____
   Is she going to bring it tomorrow night?
3 He wore it two days ago. (two days from now)_____
4 They left it the day before last. (the day after tomorrow)
   _____
5 They forgot it last week. (next week)_____
6 He wrote it a week ago yesterday. (a week from tomorrow)_____
7 She did it a month ago. (a month from now)_____
8 She sent it the week before last. (the week after next)
   _____
9 They began it yesterday afternoon. (tomorrow afternoon)
   _____

(part two)

10 They read it three days ago. (three days from now)_____
11 He shut it last night. (tomorrow night)_____
12 She drank it last week. (next week) _____
13 They drove it this week. (this week)_____
14 He said it a month ago. (a month from now)_____
15 She saw it a week ago yesterday. (a week from tomorrow)_____
16 They made it a week ago. (a week from now)_____
17 They held it the week before last (the week after next)
    _____
18 She lent it last month. (next month)_____
19 They did it the day before last. (the day after tomorrow)
    _____
20 She brought it last June. (next June)_____
21 He left it an hour ago. (an hour from now)_____
22 She wore it yesterday morning. (tomorrow morning)____
    _____
23 He sent it this year. (this year) _____
24 He wrote it a week ago Tuesday. (a week from Tuesday)
    _____
25 They took it last Thursday. (next Thursday)_____

Exercise 140 Give short answers for these questions.

(part one)

1   Are those boys from Europe?   Yes, _they are._
2   Was Tom absent yesterday?   No, _____
3   Will the men be in the living room?   No, _____
4   Did the boy move the chairs?   Yes, _____
5   Will there be a party tomorrow night?   Yes, _____
6   Do you want some coffee now?   No, _____
7   Was there a party here last night?   Yes, _____
8   Will Mary answer the phone for us?   Yes, _____
9   Are you a doctor?   No, _____
10   Will their boat arrive this afternoon?   Yes, _____
11   Is there a desk in that room?   No, _____
12   Does Mr. Smith like ice cream?   No, _____
13   Is there going to be a meeting tonight?   Yes, _____
14   Was it cool last night?   Yes, _____
15   Did the children go with her?   No, _____

(part two)

16   Did the women attend the meeting?   Yes, _____
17   Are you going to study French?   Yes, _____
18   Was Mr. Brown in the army?   Yes, _____
19   Will they travel to Norway by boat?   No, _____
20   Are you the student from Italy?   Yes, _____
21   Will the lecture be interesting?   Yes, _____
22   Were there many people at his lecture?   No, _____
23   Is there going to be a concert next week?   Yes, _____
24   Is it chilly outside right now?   No, _____
25   Will the children sleep in that bedroom?   Yes, _____
26   Did Charles find his billfold?   No, _____
27   Will this be enough money?   Yes, _____
28   Will there be enough tea for everyone?   Yes, _____
29   Was that a very difficult lesson?   No, _____
30   Does that car cost very much?   Yes, _____
31   Is the weather usually good in the spring?   Yes, _____
32   Will the policeman help us?   Yes, _____
33   Did your friend find them yesterday?   No, _____
34   Does the bus stop at this corner?   No, _____
35   Are all of the books on the shelf?   Yes, _____
36   Is that tall man in your class?   No, _____

Exercise 141   Use <u>before</u>, <u>after</u>, <u>from</u>, or <u>ago</u>.

1 They will be here a week _____ now.   _____
2 She was here the week _____ last.   _____
3 They're leaving the month _____ next.   _____
4 He finished school several years _____.   _____
5 He will return two years _____ now.   _____
6 I went to the concert the night _____ last.   _____
7 Our school ended the month _____ last.   _____
8 He left here two weeks _____ yesterday.   _____
9 I am going to go the week _____ next.   _____
10 Did you see her the day _____ yesterday?   _____
11 They are arriving a week _____ next Sunday.   _____
12 They will be here the day _____ tomorrow.   _____
13 He left for Arizona a week _____ yesterday.   _____
14 Are you going a week _____ tomorrow?   _____
15 They'll be back two days _____ now.   _____
16 She received the package a long time _____.   _____
17 Did you visit them the day _____ last?   _____

Exercise 142   Use <u>last</u>, <u>next</u>, <u>yesterday</u>, or <u>tomorrow</u>.

1 Are you going to go there _____ week?   _____
2 No, I went there _____ week.   _____
3 Did you speak to them _____ afternoon?   _____
4 No, but I'm going to do it _____ morning.   _____
5 Were they at church the week before _____?   _____
6 They won't be there the week after _____.   _____
7 Did John see you _____ morning?   _____
8 No, but I called him _____ night.   _____
9 Will you return home _____ week?   _____
10 Yes, but I'll be back the week after _____.   _____
11 Are you going to leave _____?   _____
12 No, we're leaving the week after _____.   _____
13 Will you be at home _____ night?   _____
14 No, but I'll be at home the _____ night.   _____
15 Did you write to them _____?   _____
16 No, I didn't, but I'll do it _____ morning.   _____
17 Is she going to finish the work _____?   _____
18 No, she finished it _____ night.   _____
19 Did they get it the month before _____?   _____
20 No, it didn't arrive until _____ morning.   _____

110

Exercise 143 Select the correct verb for each sentence.
Use the past tense.   Use each verb only one time.

sell
go   1 The men _went_ to the meeting.   _went_
throw   2 We _____ several letters to them.   _____
write   3 The agent _____ that old house.   _____
fall   4 They _____ to school with John.   _____
leave   5 The teacher _____ to the student.   _____
stand   6 Charles _____ his bet on the game.   _____
win   7 He _____ very tired last night.   _____
speak   8 Mr. Wilson _____ for Miami Friday.   _____
ride   9 I _____ in the line at the theater.   _____
break   10 He _____ on the ice and _____ his arm.   _____
feel   11 I _____ the ball to him. He _____ it.
catch

Exercise 144 Use <u>in</u>, <u>for</u>, <u>by</u>, or <u>until</u> in each sentence.
1 She will return _____ ten minutes.   _____
2 I'm going to stay _____ a year and a half.   _____
3 I will complete the job _____ noon tomorrow.   _____
4 They waited _____ eight.   Then they left.   _____
5 He agreed with me _____ the first time.   _____
6 Will you arrive there _____ tomorrow night?   _____
7 _____ once, I did everything correctly!   _____
8 He's not here now, but he'll be back _____ a while.   _____
9 The Browns were in Oregon _____ three years.   _____
10 _____ now, the Smiths are in Florida.   _____
11 They're going to return sometime _____ April.   _____
12 She stayed in Europe _____ some time.   _____
13 He sometimes stays _____ two or three years.   _____
14 The children stayed awake _____ eleven o'clock.   _____
15 _____ the long run, this language will help you.   _____
16 Are they going to remain there _____ a long time?   _____
17 They have left the country _____ good.   _____
18 They first came here _____ 1948.   _____
19 It will certainly be ready _____ then.   _____
20 We worked _____ six-thirty last night.   _____
21 They won't get back _____ later tonight.   _____
22 She is going to return it _____ 2:30 p.m.   _____
23 I'm going to stop _____ a few minutes now.   _____
24 They are going to return late _____ the spring.   _____
25 He's going to be there _____ quite a while.   _____

111

Exercise 145   Change these statements to questions.

1   He went to the movies. _____ *Did he go to the movies?*
2   He's going to see that movie. _____
3   She'll visit an art museum tomorrow. _____
4   Summer lasts from June until September. _____
5   He's working at the super market. _____
6   Small dogs are very popular here. _____
7   Miss Wilson is afraid of dogs. _____
8   He burned his tie with a cigarette ash. _____
9   She'll prepare lunch for us. _____
10   Mrs. White left for Seattle last night. _____
11   She'll arrive in St. Louis at noon. _____
12   They are coming over in a few minutes. _____
13   He had a good time on his vacation. _____
14   She wore her new raincoat yesterday. _____
15   You did your work very carefully. _____
16   He'll leave his overshoes in the hall. _____
17   Frank made some mistakes on the test. _____
18   They do all of their work together. _____
19   He bought some suspenders yesterday. _____
20   She has some more of them in her room. _____

Exercise 146   Change these statements to negatives.

1   Harry is going to do it. _____ *Harry isn't going to do it.*
2   I'll have enough money for that. _____
3   I understood your instructions very well. _____
4   They did the work very carefully. _____
5   I'll have ham and eggs for breakfast. _____
6   At first, we had a few problems. _____
7   The baby cried very loudly last night. _____
8   Mrs. White's husband is quite tall. _____
9   They had a little difficulty with it. _____
10   The mayor will speak about the situation. _____
11   This room has windows on two sides. _____
12   John is going to the soccer game tomorrow. _____
13   They walked along the beach together. _____
14   She told him the truth this morning. _____
15   Ed and John went to the exhibition. _____
16   That part of it is going to be tough. _____
17   They'll do that part of it for us. _____
18   The men will be back in a short while. _____

Pages 103 - 112

accept 107
afraid 112
agent 111
along 112
arm 111
army 109
art 112
ash 112
assist 106
beach 112
burn 112
clean 106
Colorado 106
complete 111
contest 106
cousin 106
Denver 106
depart 104
difficulty 107
divide 106
Ed 113
end 110
etc. 103
everyone 109
exhibition 112
group 106
hall 112
ham 112
Harry 112
husband 112
ice 111
instructions 112
line 111
living room 109
loudly 112
mayor 112
necessary 110

Norway 109
Oregon 111
overshoes 112
parents 106
part 112
phone 109
policeman 109
popular 112
prize 106
raincoat 112
remain 111
Seattle 112
September 112
situation 112
soccer 112
sometime 111
sometimes 111
St. Louis 112
super market 112
suspenders 112
tie 112
tough
while 105

husband
ice
instructions
line
livi... oom
lo...
m...
n... ry

113

LESSON ELEVEN

11A   The interrogatives *where, when,* and *why*

W h e r e   asks about the location of something.

W h e n   asks about the time of some event.

W h y   asks about the purpose or reason for an action.

The interrogative words where, when, and why require question word order.

QUESTION				SHORT ANSWER
	Is	he	going to go?	Yes, he is.
Where	is	he	going to go?	To the meeting.
When	is	he	going to go?	At eight o'clock.
Why	is	he	going to go?	Because he's the speaker.

QUESTION				SHORT ANSWER
	Did	he	take them?	Yes, he did.
Where	did	he	take them?	To his home.
When	did	he	take them?	This afternoon.
Why	did	he	take them?	Because he needed them.

11B   The interrogative word *how*

H o w   asks about [1] the manner of accomplishment; [2] the state or condition of something or somebody; [3] the extent or degree of a quality: how old, how far, how tall, how big, how small, how far (geographical distance), how long (time or length), how much, how many, etc.

The interrogative word how requires question word order.

	QUESTION			SHORT ANSWER
[1]	How	did	you do it?	With some tools.
[2]	How	is	the weather?	Pretty good.
[3]	How big	is	the room?	About ten by sixteen.

How	did	you get here?	By bus.
How	are	you today?	Fine, thanks.
How	is	the weather?	Very hot.
How	do	you like it?	Very much.
How tall	is	John?	Six feet.
How old	is	that man?	Fifty-six.
How far	is	it to Chicago?	800 miles.
How long	will	you stay?	Two months.
How long	is	that rope?	Nine yards.
How much	is	it?	Ten dollars.
How much	does	it cost?	A dollar.
How many	does	he have?	About twenty.
How many suits	does	he have?	Two or three.
How many	are	there outside?	There are two.

11C The interrogative words *whose, which,* and *what*

W h o s e   asks about ownership or relationship.

W h i c h   asks about identity, choice, or selection among a small or limited number of persons or things.

W h a t   asks about identity, choice, or selection among a large or unlimited number of persons or things.

The interrogative words whose, which, and what usually require question word order.

Whose book	did	you	read?	John's book.
Which book	did	you	read?	The top one.
What book	did	you	read?	A book about Lincoln.

Whose book	did	you	use?	
Whose books	did	you	use?	
Whose	did	you	use?	
Whose book	is	this?		John's.
Whose	is	this?		
Whose books	are	these?		
Whose	are	these?		

115

What	is	that thing?	That's a box.
What	are	those?	They're ropes.
What	are	you doing?	Nothing now.
What	do	you call this?	A "shade."
(How	do	you say that?)	(We say "fine.")
What name	did	you give him?	"William."
Which	will	he want?	That one.
Which one	do	you prefer?	This one.
Which boy	is	your brother?	The tall boy.
Which of these	is	yours	The red one.
What kind of bird	is	that?	A sparrow.
What kind of birds	are	those?	They're robins.

11D   The interrogative words *who* and *whom*

<u>Who</u>
<u>Whom</u>   ask about the identity of one person or several people.

[1]   s t a t e m e n t   w o r d   o r d e r   (<u>who</u> is the subject)

John	is	going to see	the teacher.
Who	is	going to see	the teacher?

[2]   q u e s t i o n   w o r d   o r d e r   (<u>whom</u> is the object)

			John	is	going to see	the teacher.
	*Whom	is	John		going to see	---------- ?

			John	is	going to speak	to Bob Smith.
	*Whom	is	John		going to speak	to -------- ?
To	whom	is	John		going to speak	---------- ?

* Native speakers of English very often substitute <u>who</u> for <u>whom</u> in sentences of this type. However, students have less difficulty understanding the word order of [1] and [2] if the teacher utilizes the formal distinction between the words <u>who</u> and <u>whom</u>.

Notice the difference between these pairs of questions:

Who sent it to Tom? _____ Whom did Bob send it to?
Who helped Tom today? _____ Whom did Bob help today?

The singular form of the verb is necessary in the following examples with <u>who</u> and <u>what</u>:

> I hear several voices outside.   Who <u>is</u> there?
> Who <u>is</u> going to leave the class early today?
> Tom and Bob are going now.   Who else <u>is</u> going?
> I didn't go into that room.   What<u>'s</u> in the room?

11E   The expressions *what . . . for* and *how come*

<u>What...for</u> and <u>how come</u> are conversational substitutes for <u>why</u>. Note: question word order is not necessary after the expression <u>how come</u>.

Why	are	you		studying	English?	
What	are	you		studying	English	for?
How come		you	are	studying	English?	

Why	did	you		go	there?	
What	did	you		go	there	for?
How come		you		went	there?	

11F   The expressions *how about* and *what about*

<u>How about</u> and <u>what about</u> have the same meaning and usage. Both expressions are merely question signals. They are more or less equivalent to a question mark. These expressions usually precede other questions or statements.

How about What about	the weather?	Will that affect your plans?

How about What about	Harry?	Will he get a ride with someone else?

11G   Contractions with the interrogative words

who is	=	who's
where is	=	where's
what is	=	what's

when is	=	when's
how is	=	how's

11H The indefinite *one* and *you*

<u>One</u> is an indefinite or impersonal pronoun. <u>You</u> is an informal substitute for <u>one</u>. The words <u>one</u> and <u>you</u> do not refer to a specific person. Note: the pronoun in the answer to example [2] is <u>you</u>.

[1]	How does	one	work this machine?	One	turns	it.
[2]	How do	you	work this machine?	You	turn	it.

<u>He</u>, <u>him</u>, and <u>his</u> usually refer back to <u>one</u>.

[3]	One	generally shows	his	best work to other people.
[4]	You	generally show	your	best work to other people.

11J The preposition *out of*

They moved the chair out of the room.
  (They moved it into this room.)
The man went out of the room angrily.
He took the cigarettes out of his pocket.
She looked out of the window for a long time.
He finally threw the paper out of the window.

11 L Idioms

<u>answer the phone</u>: John, please answer the phone for me.

<u>catch a cold</u>: Mrs. Brown caught a very bad cold last week.

<u>come true</u>: Did your prediction come true? It came true.

<u>out of breath</u>: Tom ran very hard. He was out of breath.

<u>out of date</u>: That's a very old catalog. It's out of date now.

<u>out of order</u>: That elevator was out of order yesterday.

<u>out of place</u>: His sly remark was very much out of place.

<u>out of sight</u>: The large airplane flew out of sight quickly.

<u>out of stock</u>: Do you have any ballpoint pens? No, I'm sorry, but they are out of stock right now.

<u>out of style</u>: That dress is quite old. It's very much out of style right now.

<u>out of the question</u>: That's definitely out of the question. It's a very ridiculous suggestion.

118

Exercise 147 Use <u>where</u>, <u>when</u>, or <u>why</u> in each sentence.

1 *Where* did you put it?   *Where*
2 _____ is the ladies' room?   _____
3 _____ do they start school again?   _____
4 _____ is it going to be ready?   _____
5 _____ was the accident last night?   _____
6 _____ is Tom studying here tonight?   _____
7 _____ did you go there just now?   _____
8 _____ will they arrive at the airport?   _____
9 _____ are you so sure about that?   _____
10 _____ do cats like fish so much?   _____
11 _____ are you going home so soon?   _____
12 _____ was he late for class this morning?   _____
13 _____ does summer start in this country?   _____
14 _____ will he be on the twenty-first of May?   _____
15 _____ did she go to the library after class?   _____

Exercise 148 Ask a question about the underlined part of each sentence. Use <u>where</u>, <u>when</u>, or <u>why</u> in each question.

1 He went <u>to the party</u>. _____ *Where did he go?*
2 It happened <u>about 4:00 p.m.</u> _____ *When did it happen?*
3 The clock is <u>above the stove</u>. _____
4 She put the cans <u>in the cupboard</u>. _____
5 The furnace is <u>in the basement</u>. _____
6 They came here <u>for a vacation</u>. _____
7 The election will be <u>in November</u>. _____
8 The chairs are <u>in the other room</u>. _____
9 He is coughing <u>because he has a cold</u>. _____
10 The accident happened <u>on Hill Street</u>. _____
11 It will be <u>at the beginning of next week</u>. _____
12 Our classes usually begin <u>at eight-thirty</u>. _____
13 There will be another meeting <u>next weekend</u>. _____
14 It's cold <u>because the furnace is out of order</u>. _____
15 Tom's birthday is <u>on the seventeenth of July</u>. _____
16 He bought his electric toaster <u>last week</u>. _____
17 They sold it <u>because they wanted a new one</u>. _____
18 He wrote to them <u>because he needed some money</u>. _____
19 We ate the cheese <u>because we were hungry</u>. _____
20 The bridge across the river is <u>near the factory</u>. _____

119

Exercise 149 Use <u>how</u>, <u>how much</u>, or <u>how many</u> in each of the following sentences.

1 _____ wide is that room?
2 _____ lemon do you want in your tea?
3 _____ expensive is that watch?
4 _____ quarts of milk do you need?
5 _____ cold is it outside now?
6 _____ questions are there in the exercise?
7 _____ do you like this city?
8 _____ is he traveling to Chicago?
9 _____ long will you stay here?
10 _____ candy did he eat yesterday?
11 _____ fast does light travel?
12 _____ do you turn on this machine?
13 _____ far is Hawaii from California?
14 _____ cups of coffee did you order?
15 _____ coffee did the men order?
16 _____ big is Mr. Brown's house?
17 _____ does one usually do that?
18 _____ oil does this furnace use?
19 _____ does one recognize his mistakes?
20 _____ workers are there in that factory?

Let's see. How do you do that one?

Exercise 150 Ask a question about the underlined part of each sentence. Begin each question with the word <u>how</u>.

1 It is <u>fifteen feet</u> wide. ___*How wide is it?*___
2 He travels <u>a great deal</u>. _____
3 There were <u>fourteen</u> people here. _____
4 I have <u>a great deal of</u> time now. _____
5 John was <u>two hours</u> late yesterday. _____
6 It isn't <u>very</u> cold outside now. _____
7 They will be there <u>for three weeks</u>. _____
8 It costs <u>about twenty-four dollars</u>. _____
9 There are <u>forty</u> floors in that building. _____
10 The table is <u>thirty-one inches</u> high. _____
11 He will come <u>within an hour</u>. _____
12 Bill saw <u>three</u> ships in the harbor. _____
13 Her brother is <u>fifty-two years</u> old. _____
14 It's <u>four hundred miles</u> to Philadelphia. _____
15 Mr. Wilson has <u>a lot of</u> money. _____
16 Detroit is <u>seven hundred</u> miles from there. _____
17 She bought <u>three</u> pairs of stockings. _____
18 The trip will cost <u>fifty-five dollars</u>.

Exercise 151 Use <u>whose</u>, <u>which</u>, or <u>what</u> in each sentence.

1 _____ time is it now?   _____
2 _____ of the books do you want?   _____
3 _____ did he say to you yesterday?   _____
4 _____ housecoat are you going to buy?   _____
5 _____ of the slips did she choose?   _____
6 _____ is Smith going to speak about?   _____
7 This book isn't mine. _____ is it?   _____
8 He has two choices. _____ will he take?   _____
9 I will use Ed's bicycle. _____ will you use?   _____
10 He isn't very popular at school. _____ is wrong?   _____
11 _____ pencil did I borrow? It isn't mine.   _____
12 _____ kind of food do you prefer?   _____
13 _____ one is he using? He has only two.   _____
14 _____ color are you painting your house?   _____
15 _____ is the common nickname for "Robert?"   _____
16 _____ of these purses belongs to Jane?   _____
17 _____ happened in your class today?   _____
18 _____ sort of thing are you looking for?   _____
19 This one is hers, but _____ is that?   _____
20 It doesn't belong to her. _____ is it?   _____

Exercise 152 Ask a question about the underlined part of each sentence. Use <u>whose</u>, <u>which</u>, or <u>what</u>.

1 She used <u>John's</u> book. _____ *Whose book did she use?*
2 That is <u>Frank's</u>. _____
3 I read <u>some magazine articles</u>. _____
4 They come from <u>Italy</u>. _____
5 That is <u>Mr. Smith's</u> house. _____
6 I borrowed <u>Bill's</u> bicycle. _____
7 They sold <u>the little</u> one. _____
8 He means <u>that</u> kind. _____
9 We rode in <u>Mr. Adams'</u> car. _____
10 She bought <u>the dress with the stripes</u>. _____
11 We studied <u>irregular verbs</u> last week. _____
12 I'm looking for <u>a hardware store</u>. _____
13 <u>The</u> one <u>in the middle</u> is mine. _____
14 <u>Mrs. Smith's</u> purse is on the chair. _____
15 The name of the book is <u>"Main Street."</u> _____

121

Exercise 153 Begin each sentence with <u>why</u>, <u>what</u>, or <u>how come</u>.

1 _____ do you prefer that one? _____
2 _____ did you do that for? _____
3 _____ did you do that? _____
4 _____ you prefer that one? _____
5 _____ did the guests leave so early? _____
6 _____ about Tom? Is he coming too? _____
7 _____ were they angry at him? _____
8 _____ he is returning to his country? _____
9 _____ did he say that? _____
10 _____ they knew all about it? _____
11 _____ did he tell them for? _____
12 _____ about us? Did he mention any names? _____
13 _____ does he want the money tomorrow? _____
14 _____ is he doing that work for? _____
15 _____ you didn't hear about it before this? _____
16 _____ do you want to get it now? _____
17 _____ about the price? Did you ask him? _____
18 _____ that dress is so expensive? _____
19 _____ is Bill doing that for? _____
20 _____ about Bob? Is he doing it too? _____
21 _____ does this exercise seem so difficult? _____
22 _____ you didn't study the lesson carefully? _____

Exercise 154 Use <u>what...for</u> instead of <u>why</u>.

1 Why did you do it? _____ *What did you do it for?*
2 Why did you come here? _____
3 Why are you here? _____
4 Why did you go home? _____
5 Why are you reading it? _____
6 Why did you go to the store? _____
7 Why were you late this morning? _____
8 Why did you go to the bank? _____
9 Why are you taking this course? _____
10 Why did you go to the library? _____
11 Why are you mad at me? _____
12 Why did she go to Europe? _____
13 Why is he writing to Mr. Wilson? _____
14 Why did they go into the office? _____

Exercise 155 Look at the answer to each question. Then complete each question with an appropriate interrogative word (<u>why</u>, <u>who</u>, <u>which</u>, <u>how far</u>, etc.).

QUESTION	ANSWER
1 _____ time is it now?	It's ten-fifteen.
2 _____ money do you have?	Ninety-five cents.
3 _____ English book is this?	It's Tom's.
4 _____ are you going now?	To the movies.
5 _____ one did he take?	The left one
6 _____ was that tall boy?	My friend, Bill.
7 _____ did you talk to?	My boss.
8 _____ is your brother?	Twenty years old.
9 _____ meat did you buy?	One pound.
10 _____ was it on the table?	I put it there.
11 _____ boy is your brother?	The tall one.
12 _____ color is his hair?	Dark brown.
13 _____ did the class elect?	The new boy.
14 _____ will she get here?	Probably Friday.
15 _____ does she come here?	Two times a year.
16 _____ did you come here?	Four months ago.
17 _____ does "crazy" mean?	It means "insane."
18 _____ do you like this food?	Very much.
19 _____ is there a bus stop?	At the next corner.
20 _____ put the chair there?	John, I think.
21 _____ he did it so quickly?	He had some help.
22 _____ about him? Is he here?	I think so.
23 _____ are you going to buy?	A new coat.
24 _____ are they talking to?	Bill Smith.
25 _____ were you in the army?	Three years.
26 _____ did you see yesterday?	Her cousin.
27 _____ do they do that for?	They enjoy it.
28 _____ is Miami from there?	Eighty miles.
29 _____ people are there here?	About twenty.
30 _____ is it to Los Angeles?	Not far.
31 _____ will you get to Boston?	By plane.
32 _____ do you travel so much?	I like it.
33 _____ will you be in Europe?	Several months.
34 _____ is your friend?	He's six feet.
35 _____ you went to Bill's?	He invited me.
36 _____ Bill and Harry?	They'll come too.

Exercise 156 Ask a question about the underlined part of each sentence. Use <u>where</u>, <u>which</u>, <u>how much</u>, etc.

(part one)

1   She lives <u>in Brooklyn</u>. _____ *Where does she live?*
2   They are <u>in the living room</u>. _____
3   That is <u>Mr. Brown's</u> briefcase. _____
4   I bought <u>one loaf of</u> bread. _____
5   She chose <u>the yellow</u> one. _____
6   He put it <u>under the table</u>. _____
7   The price is <u>eight thousand dollars</u>. _____
8   We went <u>to the movies</u> last night. _____
9   That word means <u>"fast" or "quick."</u> _____
10 I left <u>because I had a lot of work</u>. _____
11 It has <u>two hundred and fifty</u> pages. _____
12 We went at <u>twenty minutes after six</u>. _____
13 She has about <u>seventy dollars</u> with her. _____
14 We're going <u>about fifty miles per hour</u>. _____
15 He doesn't know <u>very</u> much English. _____

(Now try part two.)

(part two)

16 Chicago is <u>in the Midwest</u>. _____
17 The Browns have <u>five</u> children. _____
18 He wants <u>two</u> packages of cigarettes. _____
19 There are about <u>twenty-five</u> books here. _____
20 We call that <u>an "advertisement."</u> _____
21 The accident happened <u>at the stop light</u>. _____
22 They're <u>in the other room</u> right now. _____
23 I'm going <u>because it'll be interesting</u>. _____
24 The whole trip takes <u>about four hours</u>. _____
25 The boy <u>on the left</u> is his brother. _____
26 <u>Bill's</u> bicycle is in front of the house. _____
27 The game is going to be <u>at the stadium</u>. _____
28 We're going to look for <u>summer suits</u>. _____
29 Those are <u>Helen's</u> purse and gloves. _____
30 They're talking about <u>that last story</u>. _____
31 Charles asked Tom for <u>some money</u>. _____
32 Those men helped me <u>very</u> much last night. _____
33 <u>Mr. Wilson</u> gave Bill the papers. _____
34 We're going to spend <u>a month</u> in the mountains. _____

Exercise 157 Choose the correct word for each sentence.

1 (Why, What) did he need the money for?
2 Are there (many, much) theaters in New York?
3 We are going to a party (next, tomorrow) night.
4 Mr. Wilson still has (a few, a little) cigarettes.
5 The doctor gave (one, some) medicine to John.
6 That's Bill's car. This one is (my, mine).
7 He doesn't (ever, never) read popular novels.
8 He went to the movies (last, yesterday) night.
9 Are there (a, an, any) hard words in that story?
10 Does he have (many, much) friends at school?
11 Edward will return a week (from, after) now.
12 There weren't (many, a few) apples on the tree.
13 Mr. Brown (ever, never) eats at the cafeteria.
14 There is (a few, a little) cream in that bottle.
15 The Wilsons got back a week (before now, ago).
16 My car and (your, yours) are the same color.
17 It isn't (very, quite) hot this afternoon.
18 There is (many, much) information in that book.
19 John's brother gave (me, to me) the two keys.
20 There is (some, any) bread on his plate now.
21 They have (many, much) beautiful furniture.
22 That girl knows (a, some, a lot of) nice song.
23 The boys ate (an, many, a lot of) ice cream.
24 (Why, What) are you studying English for?
25 Is there (many, much) news in the paper tonight?
26 He doesn't have (many, much) time right now.
27 (How many, How much) times did he do that?
28 That cabinet is (too, too much) big for this room.
29 I don't have (some, any) relatives in this city.
30 There are still (several, any) sandwiches here.
31 He gave some money (John, to John) yesterday.
32 (Many, Much) people watch television every night.
33 (Why, What) is he opening the door right now?
34 (What, How) do you call that thing in English?
35 (How far, How long) is it to Mexico from here?
36 We received the letter the day (before, from) last.
37 There were (a few, a little) soldiers in the parade.
38 The big white house on the corner is (their, theirs).
39 She's going to return the week (after, from) next.

VOCABULARY FOR LESSON ELEVEN

Pages 114 - 125

above 119
accident 119
across 119
advertisement 124
again 119
angrily 118
basement 119
because 114
bicycle 121
Bob 122
boss 123
bridge 119
Brooklyn 124
brown 123
cabinet 125
can 119
cat 119
catalog 118
cents 123
choice 121
clock 119
color 121
common 121
cough 119
crazy 123
cupboard 124
department store 124
elect 123
electric 119
elevator 118
factory 119
far 114
fine 115
forty 120
fourteen 120
furnace 119
gloves 124
hair 123
happen 119

harbor 120
hardware 121
Hawaii 120
high 120
hill 119
housecoat 121
how's 117
hundred 124
insane 123
January 119
kind 121
lemon 120
loaf 124
machine 118
May 119
mention 122
the Midwest 124
mile 124
mountain 124
nickname 121
ninety 122
nothing 116
November 119
October 123
oil 120
order 120
out of 118
paint 121
parade 125
per 124
pound 123
prediction 118
prefer 121
quart 120
recognize 120
remark 118
ridiculous 118
river 119
robin 116

rope 115
seventeenth 119
seventy 124
shade 116
ship 120
sly 117
so 119
soldier 125
soon 119
sort 121
sparrow 116
stockings 120
stop light 124
stove 119
stripe 121
suggestion 118
sure 119
theater 125
thirty 120
toaster 119
tool 114
turn 117
twenty 119
under 124
weekend 119
when 114
when's 117
where 114
where's 117
which 115
who 116
whom 116
who's 117
whose 115
why 114
within 120
worker 120

LESSON TWELVE

12A   The present perfect tense

English verbs have three principal forms:

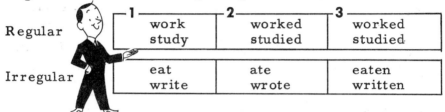

	1	2	3
Regular	work study	worked studied	worked studied
Irregular	eat write	ate wrote	eaten written

The present perfect tense uses the simple present forms of <u>have</u> + the third form (past participle) of the main verb.

1	I	have	eaten
2	you	have	eaten
3	he she it	has	eaten

we	have	eaten
you	have	eaten
they	have	eaten

The present perfect tense expresses:

[1]   an action from the past to the present. The action continues today. These expressions frequently accompany this usage: <u>since</u>, <u>for</u>, <u>yet</u>, <u>until now</u>, <u>up to now</u>, <u>for some time now</u>, <u>so far</u>.

We	have	lived	in this city since 1945.
We	have	lived	here for nine and a half years.
We	have	studied	only eleven lessons up to now.

[2]   a repeated action during the time from the past to the present.

We	have	eaten	in that restaurant several times.
We	have	been	in South America twice.
We	have	been	to France six or seven times.

127

[3] a completed action in the past.   However, the time is
    unknown.   Already frequently accompanies this usage.
Note: the expressions a long time ago, a while ago, etc. are
expressions of time and require the past tense.

We	have	eaten	our dinner already.
We	have	seen	that movie already.
We	have	finished	an elementary course in English.
We	have	learned	all of the words on the list.

[4] a completed action in the immediate past with an ex-
    pression such as at last, finally, just, etc.

| We | have | finished | that long lesson at last! |
| We | have | done | all of that work finally! |

12B Statements, questions, and negatives

	She	has		seen	the movie at that theater.
Has	she			seen	the movie at that theater?
	She	has	not	seen	the movie at that theater.

Notice the position of the frequency word in the following
example.   The words finally, already, just, etc. often
take the same position in a sentence.

	They	have		always	lived	in that house.
Have	they			always	lived	in that house?
	They	have	not	always	lived	in that house.

12C Have + got in place of have

The present perfect verb have got is a frequent substitute
for the simple present of have as a main verb.

Examples:

I've got it!

HAVE	HAVE GOT
She has a bad cold.	She has got a bad cold.
He has a lot of friends.	He's got a lot of friends.
Do you have a match?	Have you got a match?
We don't have any time.	We haven't got any time.

12C The third form of irregular verbs

be is/am/are was/were been
become — became — become
begin — began — begun
bend — bent — bent
bet — bet — bet
bite — bit — bitten
blow — blew — blown
break — broke — broken
bring — brought — brought
build — built — built
buy — bought — bought
catch — caught — caught
choose — chose — chosen
come — came — come
cost — cost — cost
cut — cut — cut
do — did — done
drink — drank — drunk
drive — drove — driven
eat — ate — eaten
fall — fell — fallen
feed — fed — fed
feel — felt — felt
find — found — found
fit — fit — fit
fly — flew — flown
forget — forgot — forgotten
get — got — got, gotten
give — gave — given
go — went — gone
grow — grew — grown
have — had — had
hear — heard — heard
hide — hid — hidden
hit — hit — hit
hold — held — held
hurt — hurt — hurt
keep — kept — kept

know — knew — known
lead — led — led
leave — left — left
lend — lent — lent
lose — lost — lost
make — made — made
mean — meant — meant
meet — met — met
pay — paid — paid
put — put — put
quit — quit — quit
read — read — read
ride — rode — ridden
run — ran — run
say — said — said
see — saw — seen
sell — sold — sold
send — sent — sent
shut — shut — shut
sing — sang — sung
sit — sat — sat
sleep — slept — slept
slide — slid — slid
speak — spoke — spoken
spend — spent — spent
spin — spun — spun
spread — spread — spread
stand — stood — stood
steal — stole — stolen
take — took — taken
teach — taught — taught
tear — tore — torn
tell — told — told
think — thought — thought
throw — threw — thrown
understand — --stood — --stood
wear — wore — worn
win — won — won
write — wrote — written

129

12D Contractions with *have* and *has*

we have	=	we've	etc.
he has	=	he's	etc.

have not	=	haven't
has not	=	hasn't

12E The prepositions *since* and *for*

SINCE   He has lived in this city since 1948.
They have been here since last week.
We have seen him only once since January.
The weather has been bad since Wednesday.
He has written two books since the war.

FOR   He has lived in this city for six years.
They have been here for five days.
She has been sick for several days now.
He studied English for five years.
He has studied English for five years.
I worked for two months last year.
The Wilsons were in Italy for a short time.
The two boys wrote letters for an hour.

Note: For is optional in many of these examples. However, by including for, the student will always be correct.

12F Idioms

as usual: As usual, John has forgotten his book. We ate at the cafeteria as usual.

each other: The two students already know each other well.

get off: I got off the bus in front of Penn Station. We often get off the subway at that stop.

get on: I usually get on the bus here. They got on the subway at nine-thirty.

get over: Did Mr. Wilson get over his cold very quickly?

get up: What time does Tom usually get up in the morning?

a great deal: Charles enjoys mystery stories a great deal.

put on: Put on your coat. It's very cold outside right now.

take off: I'm going to take off my coat. It's too hot here.

130

Exercise 158   Use the present perfect tense of the verb in each sentence.

(part one)

1   We (see) that movie. _____ *We have seen that movie.*
2   That man (cut) his hand! _____
3   She (tear) her new blouse. _____
4   The meeting (begin) already. _____
5   They (be) here for six months. _____
6   I (write) three letters to him so far. _____
7   Charles (bring) his friend with him. _____
8   Elizabeth (finish) the work already. _____
9   The Smiths (buy) a new house here. _____
10 He (fall) on these steps several times. _____
11 He (be) in this country for a long time. _____
12 They (leave) several messages for him. _____
13 The girls (thank) Mrs. Wilson for her help. ____
14 He (sell) that old car of his already. _____
15 He and the boys (reach) Houston, Texas already.__

(part two)

16 The boys (tell) him about it. _____
17 The students (do) that lesson. _____
18 Charles (have) his lunch already. _____
19 She (give) it to her sister already. _____
20 They (find) someone's billfold. _____
21 She (forget) the name of the song. _____
22 Betty and Pat (do) the dishes already. _____
23 We (follow) their directions carefully. _____
24 I (hear) that song several times already. _____
25 His English (improve) a great deal. _____
26 Mrs. Wilson (speak) to Betty about it. _____
27 So far, they (have) very good luck. _____
28 I (fly) in an airplane only two times. _____
29 Mr. Brown (teach) English for ten years. _____
30 We (spend) a great deal of money already. _____
31 They (attempt) that several times so far. _____
32 She (copy) all of the words into her notebook. __
33 Dick (take) three different courses in English. __

131

Exercise 159 Change the verbs in these sentences (a) to the past tense, (b) to the future tense, and (c) to the present perfect tense.

1 I spend my money.
        I spent my money.
        I will spend my money.
        I have spent my money.

2 They use that one. _____
3 We do it together. _____
4 He needs a new one. _____
5 They have enough time. _____
6 We pay many bills. _____
7 I do all of the lessons. _____
8 He sits in the front row. _____
9 Mr. Wilson has two cars. _____
10 Mrs. Brown translates books. _____

11 Does he eat there?
        Did he eat there?
        Will he eat there?
        Has he eaten there?

12 Do you have enough time? _____
13 Does she do the dishes? _____
14 Do you keep your books? _____
15 Does he have good luck? _____
16 Do you enjoy that work? _____
17 Do they explain it carefully? _____
18 Does he write many letters? _____
19 Does she attend the meetings? _____
20 Do you send many letters? _____

21 I don't stay there.
        I didn't stay there.
        I won't stay there.
        I haven't stayed there.

22 They don't do that work. _____
23 I don't have any energy. _____
24 He doesn't study hard. _____
25 They don't remember it. _____
26 I don't do much work here. _____
27 He doesn't review the words. _____
28 We don't discuss each lesson. _____
29 She doesn't have enough time. _____
30 He doesn't collect the money. _____
31 She doesn't do her part. _____
32 We don't see them. _____
33 He doesn't use this one. _____

132

Exercise 160   Change these statements to questions.

1   She has quit her job. _____ *Has she quit her job?*
2   He has read that article. _____
3   I have been there before. _____
4   We have never eaten there. _____
5   I have lost my new pen. _____
6   He has heard the good news. _____
7   The Smiths have built a new house. _____
8   I have never flown across the Atlantic. _____

Exercise 161   Change these statements to negatives.

1   She has finished it. _____ *She hasn't finished it.*
2   I have done that lesson. _____
3   They have bought some cigarettes. _____
4   We have learned many new words. _____
5   It has been quite warm this week. _____
6   His English has improved very much. _____
7   There have been several accidents here. _____
8   They have had a very good time. _____

Exercise 162   Use <u>since</u> or <u>for</u> in each sentence.

1   We have lived here _____ 1945. _____
2   We have lived here _____ eight years. _____
3   We lived there _____ five years before that. _____
4   They have been here _____ two months. _____
5   They have been here _____ the first of the year. _____
6   They were in Japan _____ six months last year. _____
7   She studied French there _____ one year. _____
8   Then she studied Japanese _____ a long time. _____
9   She has studied English here _____ then. _____
10   She has studied English _____ six weeks in all. _____

11   The students have been here _____ eight o'clock. _____
12   Charles worked in a shoe store _____ a year. _____
13   The weather has been good _____ last Thursday. _____
14   We stayed in Canada _____ several months. _____
15   Mr. White has lived here _____ November, 1952. _____
16   They were very busy _____ two or three hours. _____
17   I haven't seen John _____ quite a while now. _____
18   Bill hasn't been here _____ yesterday morning. _____
19   The Wilsons stayed at the hotel _____ a few days. _____
20   I haven't heard anything about it _____ the election. _____

133

Exercise 163 Make contractions if possible.

1	What is that?	21	Where is the building?
2	That is not it.	22	How is he feeling?
3	I have seen it.	23	I will not be there.
4	She is not a teacher.	24	She has not been there.
5	John does not like it.	25	That was perfect.
6	He has finished it.	26	We have written it.
7	I am not very tired.	27	That is interesting.
8	They were not there.	28	What is that thing?
9	That is not it.	29	He has already left.
10	I will not be here.	30	You are right about it.
11	They have not returned.	31	She will not be there.
12	It did not rain at all.	32	I have not heard it.
13	He does not know it.	33	Who is that man?
14	She is not a secretary.	34	I am not very busy.
15	We will not see him.	35	What is he doing now?
16	How is your English?	36	There is a book here.
17	We have not found it.	37	Where was the book?
18	She will answer it.	38	How is he going to go?
19	I do not know him.	39	This is not mine.
20	Where is your car?	40	We have not done it.

Exercise 164 Read the following selection. Then give the reason for the tense of the verb in each sentence.

MR. GREGORY

My friend Mr. Gregory [1] is studying English and French at New York University. He
[2] learned Spanish at that university three
years ago, and then he [3] went to South America for a
year. He [4] has never been to France. However, he
[5] has visited Italy several times. He [6] saw the
Coliseum during his trip to Rome in 1938. Unfortunately,
he [7] has never seen the Louvre in Paris. He [8] has
been in Africa, too. He [9] was there during the war.
He [10] started his English course last summer. Therefore, he [11] has studied English for only eight months.

134

Exercise 165 First read the answers to the incomplete questions. Then select an appropriate interrogative word (<u>where</u>, <u>who</u>, <u>how</u>, etc.) for each question.

QUESTION	ANSWER
1 _____ have you been?	At the library
2 _____ do you have?	A new toothbrush.
3 _____ did they go?	A few minutes ago.
4 _____ does the word mean?	It means "strange."
5 _____ is there?	Tom and Bill.
6 _____ are there some chairs?	In the other room.
7 _____ have they gone?	To the movies.
8 _____ did you choose?	The small one.
9 _____ kind of cloth is that?	It's silk.
10 _____ did you see them?	Yesterday.
11 _____ book is that?	Betty's.
12 _____ much does it cost?	Twenty-five cents.
13 _____ long has it been?	Two weeks.
14 _____ long ago did they leave?	Two weeks ago.
15 _____ did they leave for?	Because it was late.
16 _____ did they leave for?	Washington, D.C.
17 _____ do you like it now?	Quite well.
18 _____ are they?	George's.
19 _____ are they?	At George's (house).
20 _____ far have you gone?	Up to page 135.

Exercise 166 Ask a question about the underlined part of each sentence. Use <u>where</u>, <u>when</u>, <u>who</u>, etc.

1 She has been <u>at school</u>. _____ *Where has she been?*
2 He came back <u>at two o'clock</u>. _____
3 They have been here <u>for a week</u>. _____
4 That book belongs to <u>Elizabeth</u>. _____
5 That book costs <u>three dollars</u>. _____
6 That's <u>Charles'</u> book. _____
7 I prefer <u>the yellow</u> one. _____
8 We have <u>three or four</u> of them. _____
9 The accident happened <u>at the intersection</u>. _____
10 They gave the packages to <u>me</u>. _____
11 You pronounce that word <u>like this</u>. _____
12 We went <u>because they invited us</u>. _____
13 She chose <u>the</u> one <u>with the lace</u>. _____
14 It's about <u>ten blocks</u> to the tennis courts. _____
15 The name of that book is <u>"Tom Sawyer."</u> _____

Exercise 167 Change these statements to questions.

1 He has finished it. _____ *Has he finished it?*
2 He has many friends. _____
3 He does his lessons at home. _____
4 They never have much trouble. _____
5 She has taken two courses in Spanish. _____
6 They do the dinner dishes together. _____
7 We always have a good time there. _____
8 They are having a big sale today. _____
9 She will have enough money for it. _____
10 They are doing the last part right now. _____
11 He has always enjoyed that kind of work. _____
12 She will do that part of it for us. _____
13 They have enough food for everyone. _____
14 She did the assignment last night. _____
15 The weather has been hot for a long time. _____
16 Those women have their own books. _____
17 They have always done good work in class. _____
18 You had the right answer on your paper. _____
19 He has torn the sleeve of his coat. _____
20 Miss Wilson does her lessons carefully. _____

Exercise 168 Change these statements to negatives.

1 He has a new car. _____ *He doesn't have a new car.*
2 He has taken them. _____ *He hasn't taken them.*
3 That man has been very helpful. _____
4 This room has very many windows. _____
5 He does all of his work with me. _____
6 They are having some difficulty now. _____
7 The Smiths have a very large house. _____
8 They have taken good care of it. _____
9 She has done the lesson carefully. _____
10 They did all of the work together. _____
11 We have heard that program before. _____
12 The house had some bad features to it. _____
13 There were some very serious defects. _____
14 I have done my part of the job. _____
15 Their friend has some news about it. _____
16 We will have enough time for it. _____
17 The furniture had some scratches in it. _____
18 Those people did the work for us. _____

136

Exercise 169   Complete these idioms.

1   What time does he get --- every morning?   *(get up)*
2   --- time --- time, they go to the opera.
3   What did you do --- the meantime?
4   Why did she put --- her coat?
5   I --- your pardon! I didn't see you.
6   We went on a picnic in spite --- the cloudy weather.
7   Please take --- your coat. It's warm here.
8   From now ---, please write your exercises in ink.
9   They go --- a walk in the park now and --- .
10 Do those two boys know --- other?
11 He jumped out of the way in the --- of time.
12 Is he going to take advantage --- the offer?
13 The information in that old book is --- --- date.
14 --- course that is true! It's obvious.
15 They decided on the --- of the moment.
16 I'm leaving now. I'll turn --- the light.
17 The motor doesn't work. It's --- --- order.
18 He always pays attention --- my advice.
19 --- general, that's an interesting book.
20 The coat is old-fashioned. It's --- --- style.
21 Call the police in the event --- trouble.
22 Look --- ! There's a car behind you!
23 Charles lost his job. He's --- --- work now.
24 You will profit from that in the --- run.
25 First of --- , tell me about your trip.
26 --- usual, he has forgotten his homework.
27 Did you get --- your cold very quickly?

I did all of the sentences correctly!

137

VOCABULARY FOR LESSON TWELVE

Pages 127 - 138

advice 136
Africa 134
already 128
anything 133
attempt 131
been 127
begun 129
blown 129
broken 129
chosen 129
cloth 135
cloudy 136
the Coliseum 134
copy 131
defect 136
Dick 131
directions 131
discuss 132
done 128
driven 129
drunk 129
eaten 127
elementary 128
energy 132
fallen 129
feature 136
finally 128
flown 129
follow 131
forgotten 129
given 129
gone 129
gotten 129
grown 129
hasn't 130
haven't 130
helpful 136
hidden 129

however 134
improve 131
information 136
intersection 135
I've
known 129
lace 135
the Louvre 134
luck 131
message 131
motor 136
obvious 137
old-fashioned 136
Paris 134
past 131
Pat 131
perfect 134
picnic 136
place 133
profit 136
reach 131
ridden 129
Rome 134
row 132
scratch 136
secretary 134
seen 128
serious 136
silk 135
since 127
spoken 129
stolen 129
taken 129
tennis court 135
thank 131
therefore 134
they've 130
thrown 129

torn 129
we've 130
worn 129
written 129
you've 130

Don't 12
forget 81
these 11
new 4
words! 1

138

LESSON THIRTEEN

13A   The past tense and the present perfect tense

	She			ate	her dinner there yesterday.
Did	she			eat	her dinner there yesterday?
	She	did	not	eat	her dinner there yesterday.

	She	has		eaten	her dinner already.
Has	she			eaten	her dinner yet?
	She	has	not	eaten	her dinner yet.

THE PAST TENSE expresses a completed action at a known time in the past.

THE PRESENT PERFECT TENSE expresses [1] a continuous action from the past to the present, [2] a repeated action during the time from the past to the present, [3] a completed action at an unknown time in the past, and [4] a completed action in the immediate past with <u>finally</u>, <u>just</u>, etc.

Examples:

[1] Smith <u>lived</u> there for five years. (Then he <u>left</u>.) [2] He <u>has lived</u> here for five years. (He is living here now.) [3] Charles <u>lived</u> in Chicago from 1945 to 1950. [4] He <u>has lived</u> here since 1950. (He is here now.) [5] They <u>were</u> in Rome five years ago. [6] They <u>have been</u> in France since that time. [7] She <u>has been</u> there many times. [8] John <u>was</u> a good worker. (He is dead.) [9] John <u>has</u> always <u>been</u> a good worker. (He is still living.) [10] He <u>ate</u> lunch at 12:30. [11] He <u>has eaten</u> already. [12] Mr. Wilson <u>wrote</u> a book last year. [13] All told, Mr. Wilson <u>has written</u> four books. [14] He <u>has</u> finally <u>finished</u> all of the work! [15] They <u>have</u> just <u>spoken</u> to him about it.

13B   Negative questions

Simple question:	Is	John			in that room now?

Simple question:	Is	John			in that room now?
Simple negative:		John	is	not	in that room now.

Negative question:

type 1:	Isn't	John			in that room now?
type 2:	Is	John		not	in that room now?

Simple question:	Does	he			know	them?
Simple negative:		He	does	not	know	them.

Negative question:

type 1:	Doesn't	he			know	them?
type 2:	Does	he		not	know	them?

The negative question usually anticipates a negative answer or a reaffirmation.

Examples:

Aren't you reading it?   Didn't you speak to him?
Isn't there one here?   Won't they be there?
Don't you like it?   Won't he enjoy that?
Doesn't she know them?   Haven't you done it?
Weren't they ready?   Hasn't he seen that movie?

Both type 1 and type 2 are correct. However, type 2 is very formal. The contraction (verb + not) is necessary in type 1. Note: There is no contraction of am not. In this case, use type 2. (The form aren't I also occurs. Because of its troublesome aspects, the text does not deal with that form.)

Use this pattern with the first person singular (I):

Am I not		correct in that respect?
Am I not	doing	the work properly?
Am I not	spelling	that word correctly now?

140

13C Negative questions with why

Didn't	the student	know	the correct answer?
Why	didn't	the student	know	the correct answer?

13D Answer presuming questions

QUESTION EXPECTED ANSWER

(positive) (negative)

John is here now,	isn't he?	Yes, he is.
There is coffee left,	isn't there?	Yes, there is.
You are working now,	aren't you?	Yes, I am.
Mary walks to school,	doesn't she?	Yes, she does.
The box will be here,	won't it?	Yes, it will.
The men have seen it,	haven't they?	Yes, they have.

(negative) (positive)

The car wasn't there,	was it?	No, it wasn't.
She doesn't know it,	does she?	No, she doesn't.
The boys didn't see it,	did they?	No, they didn't.
You haven't heard it,	have you?	No, I haven't.
Smith won't like it,	will he?	No, he won't.

13E The preposition for

Review the use of for on pages 105 and 130. Also review the use of the indirect object on page 71.

[1] She spelled the word for us.
He delivered the letter to her for me.
We bought a nice gift for him.
or: We bought him a nice gift.

[2] The dress is too small for her.
Are you ready for the examination?
They always plan for the future.

[3] He went to the store for some cigarettes.
We have some candles for emergencies.
For entertainment, they played party games.

[4] He paid $75 for his new suit.
She thanked us for the present.
I need some money for the groceries.

13F Words with allied prepositions (part one)

<u>arrive at</u>: They arrived at the airport after four o'clock.

<u>arrive in</u>: She arrived in New York on the sixteenth of May.

<u>ask for</u>: I asked for a pack of cigarettes. They asked the teacher for some help.

<u>belong to</u>:   These books and papers belong to Miss Wilson.

<u>come to</u>: Many foreign students come to the United States.

<u>depend on</u>: The students depend on their teacher for help.

<u>feel sorry about</u>: George feels sorry about that mistake.

<u>feel sorry for</u>: We all feel sorry for that poor old man.

<u>go shopping for</u>: Betty Smith went shopping for a new dress.

<u>go to</u>: Many people go to Florida during the winter season.

<u>laugh at</u>: We all laughed at Mr. Brown's very funny joke.

<u>leave for</u>: When did the two boys leave for Venezuela?

<u>listen to</u>: The children listen to the radio every evening.

<u>look at</u>: We looked at the beautiful paintings by that artist.

<u>look for</u>: We all looked for Dick's pen. We finally found it.

<u>pay for</u>: How much did Mrs. Smith pay for that necklace?

<u>remind one of</u>: This city reminds me of London. That story reminded me a little of one by William Faulkner. We reminded him of his appointment in the afternoon.

<u>stay at</u>: Mr. Adams is staying at the Lincoln Hotel tonight.

<u>substitute for</u>: Mr. Foster is substituting for our regular teacher today. Please substitute this word for that one. It is a good substitute for the other one.

<u>talk about</u>: What are they talking about? They are talking about John's accident.

<u>talk to</u>: The students are talking to the teacher right now.

<u>translate from...to</u>: He is translating that book from Spanish to English.

<u>translate into</u> (or: <u>to</u>): Is he translating it into French too?

142

Exercise 170   Choose the correct verb.   Use the <u>simple present tense</u> or the <u>continuous present tense</u>.   Use each verb only one time.

cook	1	She _is playing_ the piano now.	*is playing*
seem	2	They _____ for new dresses today.	_____
know	3	Smith _____ Mr. Adams very well.	_____
smell	4	The women _____ our dinner now.	_____
need	5	Those flowers _____ very good.	_____
spell	6	Dick _____ the word for them now.	_____
see	7	We _____ John at the next corner.	_____
shop	8	I _____ some help with this exercise.	_____
have	9	That store _____ a big sale today.	_____
play	10	This lesson _____ quite easy so far.	_____

Exercise 171   Use only the <u>past tense</u> of the correct verb.

choose	1	The boy _shut_ the door quietly.	*shut*
earn	2	I ___ a pretty necktie from the pile.	_____
win	3	We _____ him of his promise.	_____
teach	4	I ___ the new student at the party.	_____
shut	5	He ___ $55 a week in that store.	_____
break	6	I ___ my bet with Frank last week.	_____
meet	7	He ___ the window with his baseball.	_____
remind	8	I ___ her the proper pronunciation of it.	_____
mention	9	He ___ your name to us several times.	_____
use	10	She _____ the new word in a sentence.	_____

Exercise 172   Use only the <u>present perfect tense</u> of the correct verb.

catch	1	The wind _has blown_ hard all day.	*has blown*
know	2	We _____ him for many years.	_____
use	3	I ___ this typewriter many times.	_____
feel	4	He ___ the number of guests carefully.	_____
copy	5	I _____ very bad for almost a week.	_____
blow	6	She ___ the words into her notebook.	_____
steal	7	Someone _____ her diamond bracelet.	_____
spend	8	The police ___ not _____ the thief yet.	_____
count	9	I ___ her by telephone several times.	_____
call	10	We ___ about $250 in the last two weeks.	_____

Exercise 173   Use the _past tense_ or the _present perfect tense_ of the verb in each sentence.

(part one)

1   We (see) that movie already. _We have seen it already_.
2   We (see) it last Tuesday night. _We saw it Tuesday night_.
3   I (read) that novel again during my vacation. _____
4   I (read) it several times before. _____
5   They (be) in Los Angeles last week. _____
6   They (be) there twice since Christmas. _____
7   He (have) a good time at the party last night. _____
8   He (have) a good time ever since his arrival. _____
9   ____you ever (eat) at that cafeteria? _____
10   ____you (eat) there the day before yesterday? _____
11   Dick ____ not (study) Russian since last spring. _____
12   He ____ not (study) French last summer either. _____
13   ____you ever (walk) across that big bridge? _____
14   No, I ____ never (walk) across it. _____
15   My friends (walk) across it two days ago. _____

(part two)

16   I (finish) the work about two hours ago. _____
17   I (have) little trouble with this up to now. _____
18   We (travel) by air many times in the past. _____
19   The Browns (leave) for Arizona a week ago. _____
20   ____you ever (see) the Louvre in Paris? _____
21   It (snow) every day this past week. _____
22   ____you (visit) the Eiffel Tower during your vacation? __
23   Mr. Gregory (come) here in 1948. _____
24   We (be) in New York twice last month. _____
25   How long ago ____you (deliver) the package? _____
26   Our present teacher (live) here all of his life. _____
27   Ralph (make) much progress since July. _____
28   ____ she (send) the telegram this morning? _____
29   Where ____ you (be) since last summer? _____
30   When ____ you (go) on your trip? _____
31   ____they (enjoy) everything here so far? _____
32   ____they (learn) all of the new words yesterday? _____
33   Up to now, he (do) very good work. _____
34   I (have) a little trouble with it last week. _____
35   However, I (have) no trouble since then. _____

144

Exercise 174 Use only the words since, for, ago, in, on, and at in these sentences.

A BRIEF HISTORY OF A. F. ROSSI

Mr. Rossi was born ____ Genoa, Italy. He was born ____ March 15, 1907 ____ midnight. He lived ____ Genoa ____ eight years. Then he moved to Rome ____ 1915. He fell in love with that city, and he has written a lot of stories about Rome ____ that time. However, it has been quite a long time ____ his last year ____ that city. He went to school ____ Rome ____ ten years. He quit school ____ June, 1925. Then he worked ____ a large newspaper ____ France ____ five years. Mr. Rossi came to the United States ____ the spring of 1930. He became a citizen ____ the twentieth of April, 1935. He has had a house ____ this city ____ that time. ____ all, he has lived ____ this country ____ quite a long time. Mr. Rossi took a course ____ English a number of years ____. He started this course ____ ten o'clock ____ the morning ____ October 7, 1935. He studied English ____ two years. He has also studied German and Spanish ____ that time. He studied German ____ the summer of 1940, and he started his Spanish course ____ February 3, 1943. He studied this language ____ three years. Mr. Rossi went to South America six years ____, and he stayed there ____ two years. Then he returned to the United States ____ good. He has also written many things about South America ____ that trip. Mr. Rossi has been a professional writer ____ his first job ____ the French newspaper. He wrote his first article ____ 1925. ____ then, he has written almost 800 articles and stories.

Exercise 175 Give the correct form of the verb for each sentence on "A Brief History of A. F. Rossi."

1 Mr. Rossi (be) born in the year 1907. _____
2 He (write) almost eight hundred articles. _____
3 He first (come) to this country in 1930. _____
4 He (live) in the United States since 1930. _____
5 He (study) the German language in 1940. _____
6 He (start) his Spanish course a few years later. _____
7 He (return) from South America after two years. _____
8 He (be, never) to Canada or Alaska. _____
9 He (leave) Genoa, Italy after eight years. _____
10 He (study) two languages since 1940. _____
11 He (take) an English course in October, 1935._____
12 He (live) in this country for a long time. _____
13 He (study) German for three months. _____
14 He (have) a house here since 1932. _____
15 He (be) a professional writer since 1925. _____

Exercise 176 Give a complete answer to each question on "A Brief History of A. F. Rossi."

1 What year was Mr. Rossi born in? *He was born in 1907.*
2 How long ago was he born? _____
3 How long did he live in Genoa? _____
4 How long did he go to school in Rome? _____
5 How long has he been in this country? _____
6 How many years ago did he leave France? _____
7 When did he leave for South America? _____
8 Where did Mr. Rossi go in 1925? _____
9 When did he finish his English course? _____
10 In what year did he finish the Spanish course? _____
11 How many languages does he know in all? _____
12 When did he become a citizen of this country? _____
13 How many years has he been a writer? _____
14 When did he return to the United States for good? _____
15 In all, how many articles has he written? _____
16 Where was Mr. Rossi five years ago? _____
17 Where is he going to go next? _____
18 When did he quit school in Rome? _____
19 How many years ago did he leave Italy? _____
20 How many years has he spoken English? _____
21 How old is Mr. A. F. Rossi today? _____

Exercise 177   Add negatives to these questions.

1   Is his book on the desk? ____*Isn't his book on the desk?*____
2   Did the boys go to the movies? _____
3   Will Bill be at the party tomorrow? _____
4   Have you written the letter yet? _____
5   Are they leaving for Europe next week? _____
6   Is John going to go home after school? _____
7   Did Mr. Smith walk to school today? _____
8   Are there any chairs in the other room? _____
9   Will they arrive here on Saturday? _____
10 Has she ever watched a baseball game? _____
11 Are there any shelves in this closet? _____
12 Have Tom and John seen that yet? _____
13 Did he wear his new sport coat yesterday? _____
14 Do those doctors like American food? _____
15 Is his plane arriving this afternoon? _____

Exercise 178   Change these statements to negative questions.

1   He is in his office now. ____*Isn't he in his office now?*____
2   The men studied the lesson. _____
3   Mr. Wilson never drinks coffee. _____
4   There were some pictures on the wall. _____
5   She is going to go to the movies tonight. _____
6   They will arrive in Los Angeles tomorrow. _____
7   Harry has never been in Costa Rica. _____
8   Foster borrowed his friend's book. _____
9   That lawyer will be in our class tomorrow. _____
10 Mr. Brown was at the meeting yesterday. _____
11 We have finished all of the work. _____
12 There is some milk in the bottle. _____
13 Betty wore her new dress to the party. _____
14 It was a very easy assignment. _____
15 He bought some new shoes yesterday. _____
16 It will be ready for us by then. _____
17 They knew the answers to the questions. _____
18 Miss Wilson is leaving for England on Friday. _____
19 The people have had a very good time there. _____
20 She does all of her work very carefully. _____
21 That store is having a big sale today. _____
22 Dick will be here in time for the meeting. _____

147

Exercise 179 Add <u>why</u> to these negative questions.

1 Isn't he in town today? _____ *Why isn't he in town today?*
2 Aren't you studying now? _____
3 Wasn't he in class yesterday? _____
4 Won't he be in his office tomorrow? _____
5 Didn't they go to the meeting? _____
6 Haven't you eaten lunch yet? _____
7 Doesn't he like sandwiches? _____
8 Weren't there any sandwiches? _____
9 Won't there be a meeting on Friday? _____
10 Hasn't she heard the news yet? _____
11 Don't you understand the question? _____
12 Didn't you go there with the lawyer? _____
13 Doesn't George know this word? _____
14 Wasn't the package ready for him? _____
15 Haven't they returned it to him yet? _____

Exercise 180 Ask questions with <u>why</u> about these negative statements.

1 He wasn't in his office. _____ *Why wasn't he in his office?*
2 She didn't write the letter. _____
3 Dick isn't using his book now. _____
4 She hasn't done that work yet. _____
5 The doctors weren't at the meeting. _____
6 Charles didn't get to work on time. _____
7 That man didn't go with the other people. _____
8 Gregory hasn't enrolled at the university yet. _____
9 There weren't any students in the library. _____
10 He isn't going to go to Europe this year. _____
11 There won't be any food in the refrigerator. _____
12 Bill hasn't done that work yet. _____
13 Your papers weren't on my desk this morning. _____
14 The women didn't understand that lesson. _____
15 Mr. Johnson didn't read the assignment. _____
16 I haven't spoken to Professor Taylor yet. _____
17 She wasn't in the room at the time. _____
18 He hasn't had any time for that. _____
19 They didn't do their share of the work. _____
20 We haven't heard anything from them yet. _____
21 His wife didn't agree with them. _____
22 Mr. Wilson hasn't given us an answer. _____

Exercise 181 Complete these answer presuming questions.
Also give the expected short answer to each question.

1   The sun is shining now, *isn't it?*   *Yes, it is.*
2   Mr. Brown lives in New York, *doesn't he?*   _____
3   John hasn't come back yet, _____ _____
4   They weren't in the office, _____ _____
5   Miss Wilson speaks Russian well, _____ _____
6   There aren't any people there, _____ _____
7   Mrs. Smith doesn't have a car, _____ _____
8   The boys have friends here, _____ _____
9   There haven't been any fires, _____ _____
10   Mr. Brown went home very late, _____ _____
11   The men didn't see you, _____ _____
12   He hasn't written the letter yet, _____ _____
13   Frank will come to our house, _____ _____
14   He studies each vocabulary list carefully, ____ _____
15   Your friend has got a new suit, _____ _____
16   You don't have any free time now, _____ _____
17   Dick is going to go tomorrow, _____ _____
18   They have enough money now, _____ _____
19   Your aunt has returned from Canada, _____ _____
20   That lesson is very difficult, _____ _____
21   There were some keys on the desk, _____ _____
22   Charles and Pat are there now, _____ _____
23   The men do their work together, _____ _____
24   You didn't leave the door open just now, ____ _____
25   The Browns aren't eating right now, _____ _____
26   There wasn't any coffee in the pot, _____ _____
27   That lawyer will be at the meeting, _____ _____
28   The Wilsons arrive here tomorrow, _____ _____
29   Those women have already seen it, _____ _____
30   These aren't your cigarettes, _____ _____
31   There will be enough coffee, _____ _____
32   The workers haven't done that part yet, ____ _____
33   That has been a lot of trouble for you, ____ ____
34   Four or five of them agreed with us, ____ __
35   The children don't make much noise, ____ __
36   These new words are not difficult, _____
37   That bus goes to Washington Square, ____
38   He is not at New York University now, ____
39   He graduated from there last year, _____
40   The lock did not work properly, _____

149

Exercise 182 Use the correct preposition in each sentence.

(part one)

1 We are talking ____ the last lesson.. ____
2 I looked ____ a new apartment and finally found one. ____
3 He has worked ____ that company ____ the war. ____
4 The plane will arrive ____ the airport ____ five minutes. ____
5 It isn't a good substitute ____ the other one. ____
6 We'll be ____ Detroit ____ June ____ August. ____
7 Brown won't be back here ____ quite a while. ____
8 They always depend ____ our assistance. ____
9 He's translating his last book ____ French now. ____
10 That kind of coat is very much ____ style this year. ____
11 She is shopping ____ a new spring hat now. ____
12 There were ____ least a hundred people here. ____
13 We're going to stay there ____ noon tomorrow. ____
14 ____ whom do these gold earrings belong? ____
15 ____ general, you are probably right about that. ____

(part two)

16 I'll wait right here ____ five o'clock. ____
17 I haven't seen Tom ____ all ____ last Tuesday. ____
18 We felt very sorry ____ that poor family. ____
19 They were ____ New Mexico ____ a while last year. ____
20 She went ____ the super market ____ some groceries. ____
21 The bus will leave the station ____ ten minutes. ____
22 When did the Smiths arrive ____ Miami, Florida? ____
23 We gave a big party ____ them last weekend. ____
24 Is she going to stay ____ Louisiana ____ September? ____
25 Many tourists come ____ this city ____ the winter. ____
26 What time did you arrive ____ the train station? ____
27 The doctor's office hours are ____ ten ____ four-thirty. ____
28 This suit is much too heavy ____ summer wear. ____
29 The post office and that clinic are ____ the same street. ____
30 They aren't going to stay ____ England ____ very long. ____
31 The motor won't run. It's ____ ____ order now. ____
32 We thanked them ____ their help in the matter. ____
33 ____ whom is he talking ____ that now? ____
34 ____ the end, they decided ____ something else. ____
35 The men went ____ a walk ____ the park. ____
36 ____ time ____ time, we go there. ____
37 It doesn't work! It's ____ ____ order. ____

150

Pages 139 - 150

Alaska 146
appointment 142
Arizona 144
artist 142
assistance 150
author 146
born 145
bracelet 143
candle 141
Christmas 144
clinic 150
Costa Rica 147
dead 139
depend 142
diamond 143
earn 143
earrings 150
the Eifel Tower 144
either 144
else 150
emergency 141
enroll 148
entertainment 141
exact 146
Faulkner, William 142
free 149
foreign 142
Foster 142
gold 150
graduate 149
Harry 147
initial 146
keys 149
London 142
matter 150
pile 143
pot 149

professional 145
promise 143
pronunciation 143
proper 143
properly 140
regular 142
respect 140
Russian 144
sale 143
share 148
shelves 147
sport coat 147
substitute 142
telegram 144
tourist 150
twice 144
vocabulary 149
writer 145

151

LESSON FOURTEEN

14A   The words *no* and *not*

The word <u>no</u> never precedes: <u>a</u>, <u>an</u>, <u>the</u>, <u>any</u>, <u>much</u>, <u>many</u>, <u>enough</u>. English sentences require only one nega-tive word. However, answers do not always follow this rule. Study the following expressions with <u>no</u> and <u>not</u>:

[1]   We have <u>no</u> money in the bank now.
      We do <u>not</u> have any money in the bank now.

[2]   There are <u>no</u> books in the bookcase.
      There are <u>no</u> English books in the bookcase.
      There are <u>not</u> any books in the bookcase.

[3]   <u>No</u> students were at that meeting.
      <u>Not</u> many students were at that meeting.

[4]   Do you like coffee at all?   <u>No</u>, I do<u>n't</u>.
      Did<u>n't</u> you finish it?   <u>No</u>, I didn't.

[5]   Do<u>n't</u> you want this?   <u>Not</u> at all.
      Wo<u>n't</u> you be mad at us?   <u>Not</u> in the least.
      Are<u>n't</u> you going to go?   <u>Not</u> right now.
      Who took my book?   <u>Not</u> I.

[6]   Please answer "yes" or "<u>no</u>" to the question.

[7]   Are you going to go with them <u>or not</u>?
      Did Tom and Bill like that movie <u>or not</u>?

[8]   Those students speak Portuguese, <u>not</u> Spanish.
      Football, <u>not</u> baseball, is my favorite sport.

14B   The expressions *still, any more,* and *any longer*

	That boy	is	still	a student.	
Is	that boy		still	a student?	
	That boy	isn't		a student	any more. any longer.

	That boy		still	works	here.	
Does	that boy		still	work	here?	
	That boy	doesn't		work	here	any more. any longer.

152

Still indicates a continuation without change. Still takes the same position as the word always except in negatives:

| Mr. Moore | still | doesn't agree with me. |

Any more and any longer indicate a discontinuance of something. These words occur only in negative sentences. Both words occur at the end of the sentence.

14C   The words *already* and *yet*

It's early, but the man	is	already	here.	
It's early, but the man	is		here	already.
It's late , but the man	isn't		here	yet.

It's early, but the man	has	already	arrived.	
It's early, but the man	has		arrived	already.
It's late , but the man	hasn't		arrived	yet.

Already expresses a time earlier or shorter than the speaker or another person expected. Already does not occur in negative sentences. Notice the two positions for already.

·Yet expresses a time later or longer than the speaker or another person expected. Yet (with this meaning) does not occur in statements. Yet occurs at the end of the sentence.

Both already and yet occur in questions. In questions, the word already implies surprise on the part of the speaker.

| Has the meeting started   yet? | It's getting late! |
| Has the meeting started already? | It's only 7:30 p. m. |

14D   The words *also, too,* and *either*

| Example [1] | Bob likes music. Frank likes music too. |
| Example [2] | Frank likes music. Frank likes art too. |

Too and also have the same meaning in examples [1] and [2]. Both words occur in statements and questions. Also has two possible positions in a sentence. Too and either occur only at the end of the sentence.

Miss Wilson	is	also	a very good student.	
Miss Wilson	is		a very good student	also. too.
Miss Wilson	isn't		a very good student	either.

Mrs. Williams		also	likes	music.	
Mrs. Williams			likes	music	also. too.
Mrs. Williams	doesn't		like	music	either.

14E Short additions with *too* and *either*

In example [1] of the previous section (14D), the addition often takes a short form. Also is an exact substitute for too in these short additions. Either occurs only in negative additions.

Statement:	Charles	is	in the other room.	
Full addition:	John	is	in the other room	too.
Short addition:	John	is		too.

Statement:	Charles	likes	music and art.	
Full addition:	John	likes	music and art	too.
Short addition:	John	does		too.

Examples:

Tom knew the answer. Bill did too.
Tom didn't know the answer. Bill didn't either.
She will be at the conference. We will too.
We haven't seen him yet. I haven't either.
Frank is going to go. Is Tom too?
John works very hard. Does Bill too?

14F Words with allied prepositions (part two)

absent from: Mr. Wilson was absent from the last meeting.

accustomed to: We are not accustomed to this climate yet.

afraid of: Miss Brown is very much afraid of black cats.

associate with: He associates with those men a great deal.

154

borrow from: They borrowed some money from George. He borrowed from absolutely everyone.

call attention to: Frank called my attention to that matter.

care for: [1] I don't care for that dress at all.   [2] That hospital cares for very old people.

careful of (or: about, with):   We will be very careful of it.

certain of (or: about):   I'm not very certain of that just yet.

close to: That thin man close to John is my uncle.   The bookcase is close to the couch.

consist of: The group consists of two doctors and a lawyer.

contrary to: That is contrary to your previous statement.

decide on: Have you decided on a date for your wedding?

except for: He knows all of them except for that tall man.

familiar with: He is quite familiar with European customs.

famous for: That man is famous for his wonderful paintings.

find fault with: Mr. Foster often finds fault with her work.

fond of: He's fond of that girl.   Are you fond of strong tea?

full of: That pint bottle is full of milk.   The room is full of people now.   He's full of energy today.

insist on: I insisted on my rights.   We insist on an answer!

interested in: Are you still interested in that same subject?

known as: He is known as an author all over the world.

known for: That restaurant is known for its wonderful food.

next to: The Smiths live right next to Mr. and Mrs. Brown.

plenty of: There are plenty of cigarettes here for both of us.

put up with: How do you put up with his very poor manners?

suspicious of (or: about):   We're very suspicious of that man.

sure of (or: about):   Are you sure of that?   I'm not sure of it.

take care of: Take good care of that for me, won't you?

worry about: Don't worry about that.   It will be all right.

EXERCISES FOR LESSON FOURTEEN

Exercise 183 Complete these sentences with <u>no</u> or <u>not</u>.

1 There are _*no*_ chairs here.   *no*
2 Mr. Johnson does _*not*_ have a car.   *not*
3 English is ____ a very difficult language.   _____
4 Smith is ____ in his office right now.   _____
5 There were ____ mistakes on your paper.   _____
6 I hear____ difference between those sounds.   _____
7 We did ____ have any new words yesterday.   _____
8 Has he finished the job or ____?   _____
9 That will be too much work. -- ____at all.   _____
10 There's ____ much orange juice in the bottle.   _____
11 There's ____ time like the present. (proverb)   _____
12 Did you say anything to him? -- ____one word!   _____
13 Have you spoken to Mr. Smith or ____?   _____
14 ____ many rooms have good ventilation.   _____
15 ____ person here speaks Japanese.   _____
16 ____ much music comes over that station.   _____
17 ____ news is good news. (proverb)   _____

Exercise 184 Add <u>still</u> or <u>any more</u> to each sentence.

1 Is he at school?_____ *Is he still at school?*
2 Mr. Foster is at the meeting. _____
3 She isn't studying French. _____
4 They are living in Detroit. _____
5 Is Frank working at that store? _____
6 No, he doesn't work there. _____
7 I work at the drugstore. _____
8 He's got the same trouble. _____
9 Is it raining outside? _____
10 No, it isn't raining. _____
11 Do you like to play tennis? _____
12 He isn't the president of that company. _____
13 We are in the same English class. _____
14 Does Mr. Johnson smoke cigars? _____
15 John is studying the last lesson._____
16 That student isn't in this class._____
17 You need much more practice. _____
18 She's got a very bad accent. _____
19 They will be in the same place._____
20 We don't have the same one._____

Exercise 185   Use <u>already</u> or <u>yet</u> in each sentence.

1   The man hasn't arrived _____.
2   The meeting has _____ started.
3   Mr. Johnson has spoken to them _____.
4   The men were _____ in the room.
5   You haven't done that work ____, have you?
6   You have finished it _____, haven't you?
7   Have you heard the good news _____?
8   He's had no opportunity for that ____.
9   Miss Williams is _____ a member, isn't she?
10 Her friend hasn't joined the club____, has she?
11 All of the guests have gone home _____.
12 Not very many people know that _____.
13 They've ____ had their new car for a week.
14 No one has given the correct answer to it ____.
15 They have had no time for that _____.
16 Oh yes, they've had plenty of time _____.
17 We have learned quite a bit of English _____.
18 We haven't started with the advanced book ____.

Exercise 186   Use <u>yet</u> or <u>still</u> in each sentence.

1   He hasn't finished the work _____.
2   Does John _____ work at the same store?
3   Have you spoken to Mr. Brown _____?
4   Are the men _____ at their office?
5   We _____ live in the same apartment.
6   Has she learned all of the new words _____?
7   Your vocabulary is _____ much too small.
8   He hasn't done the work _____, has he?
9   They haven't heard the good news _____.
10 He is _____ working on that machine.
11 Haven't you done the dinner dishes _____?
12 Miss Wilson hasn't been there _____, has she?
13 Mr. White_____ goes to work by bus.
14 Is it _____ raining very hard outside?
15 Haven't you had any time for that _____?
16 Don't you know the answer to that question ____?
17 Do you _____ think so?
18 Are there _____ a few people inside?
19 Your friend is _____ in the army, isn't he?
20 They probably haven't arrived at the station ___.

157

Exercise 187 Add <u>still</u> or <u>yet</u> to each sentence.

1 Is it snowing outside? _____*Is it still snowing outside?*
2 It hasn't stopped snowing. _____
3 Do you enjoy the snow after this weather? _____
4 Are you studying economics at the same school? _____
5 Have you taken any courses in law? _____
6 Don't you know anything about courts? _____
7 Are you worrying about the same thing? _____
8 Tom is working for the Department of Agriculture. ____
9 He hasn't found a new position. _____
10 Does he make the same salary? _____
11 We're living in New York. _____
12 Haven't you bought a house? _____
13 No, we're living in the same apartment. _____
14 Have you looked for a new house? _____
15 No, we don't have enough money. _____
16 Haven't you saved enough money for one? _____

Exercise 188 Add <u>too</u> or <u>either</u> to each sentence.

1 We like warm weather *too* .   *too*
2 He didn't memorize the new words *either*.   *either*
3 That doctor is from Europe _____ .   _____
4 They didn't go to the symphony concert _____ .   _____
5 That subject is quite interesting _____ .   _____
6 They haven't had any time _____ .   _____
7 We have seen that museum _____ .   _____
8 They saw the famous statue _____ .   _____
9 Mr. Smith doesn't smoke cigars _____ .   _____
10 Miss Foster is studying Spanish _____ .   _____
11 Have you been in Europe _____ ?   _____
12 Haven't those people been in Europe _____ ?   _____
13 They're in the other room _____ .   _____
14 Brown isn't reading the newspaper _____ .   _____
15 The children watched television _____ .   _____
16 You have done that _____ , haven't you?   _____
17 She hasn't done that _____ , has she?   _____
18 He's going to go to the show with us _____ .   _____
19 No one else has done it _____ .   _____
20 They won't be at the conference _____ .   _____
21 Not many people care for that _____ .   _____
22 Mr. Smith is an American citizen _____ .   _____
23 Haven't you finished your work _____ ?   _____

Exercise 189 Change these statements to negatives.

1 John likes coffee too. _John doesn't like coffee either._
2 They are at the meeting also. _____
3 Are you going to visit the museum too? _____
4 Have you also visited Central Park? _____
5 He also likes baseball and football. _____
6 Mr. Garcia is from South America also. _____
7 Has Mr. Johnson also heard about it? _____
8 We went to the World Series too. _____
9 He's studying Latin and Greek too. _____
10 We still enjoy tennis too. _____
11 Will they be at the conference too? _____
12 She also likes hot dogs. _____
13 They have some money with them too. _____
14 We are learning Russian also. _____
15 He's also got some Cuban stamps. _____
16 She plays the violin also. _____
17 They still have some tickets too. _____

Exercise 190 Complete these short additions with <u>too</u> or <u>either</u> and a verb if necessary.

1 John is very tired. I am ____.
2 They're studying the lesson. He is ____.
3 Smith wasn't at work yesterday. I wasn't ____.
4 She didn't walk to work. They didn't ____.
5 He isn't going to the meeting, and I'm not ____.
6 He read the article carefully, and she _____.
7 They haven't done it yet, and we _____.
8 She didn't know that word, and I _____.
9 I have already found one, and he _____.
10 They weren't very busy, and we _____.
11 She bought a new dress, and I _____.
12 We haven't had enough time yet, and she _____.
13 The two women listened to it, and we _____.
14 I fell on that slippery spot, and they _____.
15 She has already been there, and we _____.
16 We're going to go next week, and John _____.
17 Not many people heard the speech, and I _____.
18 Mr. Wilson won't see him, and we _____.
19 They spoke to Mrs. Smith, and Betty _____.
20 No one else enjoys it, and we _____.
21 He put his on the table, and I _____.

159

Exercise 191   Make short additions to these sentences.

1	I like sandwiches.	He	*does too.*
2	They aren't working now.	We	*aren't either.*
3	We went to the movies.	She	_____
4	She wasn't at the party.	Bill	_____
5	He's already done it.	We	_____
6	We'll visit that museum.	They	_____
7	I don't like coffee at all.	Betty	_____
8	I'm going to go tomorrow.	She	_____
9	They haven't had any trouble.	Brown	_____
10	We know Smith very well.	She	_____
11	I won't be there tomorrow.	Tom	_____
12	We haven't found one yet.	They	_____
13	Wilson isn't in his office.	Smith	_____
14	She's been there several times.	We	_____
15	They sold their old books.	He	_____

Exercise 192   Add the indicated words to these sentences.

1 (always) Is that true? _____ *Is that always true?*
2 (either) I didn't mail my application. _____
3 (still) Do you find this language simple? _____
4 (ever) Have they visited that national park? _____
5 (too) Mr. Foster bought a leather briefcase. _____
6 (yet) Are you accustomed to our climate? _____
7 (never) He has been to Belgium. _____
8 (him) We sent a very practical gift. _____
9 (often) His brother stays here over the weekend. _____
10 (either) He didn't finish his part, did he? _____
11 (still) There are plenty of sandwiches here. _____
12 (usually) We use that word this way. _____
13 (too) Bill needs some new clothes. _____
14 (to her) I mailed the letter several days ago. _____
15 (always) He does his work at the last minute. _____
16 (yet) I haven't found a solution to the problem. _____
17 (seldom) We go to that section of the city. _____
18 (either) They didn't notice anything unusual. _____
19 (to us) She didn't explain the assignment. _____
20 (always) Are their teachers very strict? _____
21 (generally) Does John do his part of it? _____
22 (always) Have you been interested in that subject? _____
23 (already) You've done that part, haven't you? _____

Exercise 193   Supply the correct preposition.

on   with   for   about

1   Are you sure _____ that? _____
2   He doesn't care _____ any dessert. _____
3   Are you familiar _____ that textbook? _____
4   That's quite contrary _____ the truth. _____
5   Mr. Brown always worries _____ everything. _____
6   They arrived _____ the airport _____ noon. _____
7   Except _____ Bill, everyone went _____ the picnic. _____
8   I asked the clerk _____ some medical supplies. _____
9   They borrowed some money _____ Charles. _____
10 They'll arrive _____ Los Angeles _____ six-thirty. _____
11 Are you accustomed _____ the food here yet? _____
12 Are you staying _____ the Lincoln Hotel? _____
13 The bank is very close _____ the post office. _____
14 Did you call Brown's attention _____ that? _____
15 The garage is right next _____ the house. _____
16 Many northerners go _____ California _____ the winter. _____
17 He always finds fault _____ other people's work. _____
18 Do they ever listen _____ classical music? _____
19 That university is famous _____ its medical school. _____
20 What subject did Mr. Wilson talk _____? _____
21 Is he interested _____ stamp collecting? _____
22 When are you leaving _____ Ecuador? _____
23 _____ whom does that large house belong? _____
24 Betty is quite fond _____ chocolate candy. _____
25 This is only a substitute _____ the other one. _____
26 That depends _____ many different things. _____
27 She translates books _____ German _____ English. _____
28 They are talking _____ the teacher _____ it now. _____
29 I'm not certain _____ the name _____ that book. _____
30 How much are you going to pay _____ the house? _____
31 All of us feel very sorry _____ you. _____
32 The police are very suspicious _____ that man. _____
33 The teacher won't put up _____ his behavior any more. _____
34 Don't be afraid _____ the dog. He won't bite you. _____
35 His brother explained the details _____ us carefully. _____
36 They insisted _____ an immediate answer. _____
37 She was absent _____ the conference _____ two hours. _____
38 The pail is completely full _____ water now. _____
39 That company is known _____ its very fine work. _____
40 How many parts does the examination consist _____? _____

161

Exercise 194 Use the correct tense of each verb.

He has written the letter already.

1 He (write) the letter already. _____
2 I (sleep) very well last night. _____
3 Please (stop) that noise right away! _____
4 We (spend) some time there last year. _____
5 He (paint) his house a week from Friday. _____
6 I (improve) very much since September. _____
7 I (study) there for a year. I (study) here now. _____
8 They (sell) their house several days ago. _____
9 The Browns (go) there every now and then. _____
10 I (forget) that man's name already. _____
11 (Look up) that word in your dictionary, please. _____
12 Our instructor (teach) us that last time. _____
13 The weather (be) terrible since Monday. _____
14 He always (like) some coffee after dinner. _____
15 They (speak) to her several times already. _____
16 She (agree) with us about that last night. _____
17 Charles (need) some money right away. _____
18 They (return) to Cuba a week from today. _____
19 It (grow) a little bit since last year. _____
20 Listen! I (hear) someone outside. _____

Exercise 195 Ask a question about the underlined part of
each sentence. Use the words <u>why</u>, <u>what</u>, <u>how</u>, etc.

1 I want <u>that</u> one. _____ *Which one do you want?*
2 He's going <u>on the fourteenth</u>. _____
3 She gave me <u>a lot of</u> information. _____
4 They're going to go <u>to Peru</u>. _____
5 The bald man is <u>Mr. White's brother</u>. _____
6 They'll come back <u>by train</u>. _____
7 They'll return <u>shortly after Labor Day</u>. _____
8 She put it <u>in the cabinet</u>. _____
9 That is <u>the Wilsons'</u> car. _____
10 They went <u>because it was late</u>. _____
11 This room is <u>twenty-one feet</u> wide. _____
12 She left here <u>the day before last</u>. _____
13 That is <u>Frank Foster's</u>. _____
14 It takes <u>four hours</u> from here to there. _____
15 He speaks <u>Portuguese and Spanish</u>. _____
16 There are <u>quite a few</u> difficult sections. _____

Exercise 196   Select the correct verb for each sentence Use the <u>simple present tense</u> or the <u>continuous present tense</u>.   Use each verb only once.

move	1	We _learn_ a lot of words every week.	_learn_
talk	2	They ———— the furniture right now.	————
admire	3	He always ——his car slowly.	————
drive	4	They ———— their overcoats now.	————
deserve	5	She ———— her grandmother this week.	————
visit	6	He ———— them a funny story right now.	————
✓learn	7	He ——about his war experiences now.	————
look	8	You ———— credit for your effort.	————
tell	9	I always ————someone like that.	————
take off	10	They ———— at the photographs now.	————

Exercise 197   Use only the <u>past tense</u> of these verbs.

melt	1	He _finished_ it an hour ago.	_finished_
sleep	2	I ———— for eight hours last night.	————
wear	3	Who ————the food for the picnic?	————
✓finish	4	He——in a high school for two years.	————
employ	5	The dog ———— over the fence.	————
teach	6	The snow ———— very rapidly.	————
furnish	7	The children ———— the records.	————
break	8	——you —— the car doors?	————
jump	9	The company——twenty men last year.	————
lock	10	Pat ———— her new dress yesterday.	————

Exercise 198   Use only the <u>present perfect tense</u>.

know	1	He _has learned_ those words.	_has learned_
talk	2	We ————Wilson for many years.	————
break	3	I ———— my hand!	————
write	4	He ——to me about it several times.	————
leave	5	They——him the package already.	————
be	6	I——never —— in that store before.	————
give	7	He——several books about chemistry.	————
✓learn	8	The boys ———— for Boston already.	————
hurt	9	We ——that assignment already.	————
do	10	The boys ——the glass in the window.	————

VOCABULARY FOR LESSON FOURTEEN

Pages 152 - 163

absolutely 155
accent 155
accustomed 155
admire 163
agriculture 158
also 153
associate 155
bald 162
behavior 161
Belgium 160
black 155
bookcase 152
care 155
certain 155
chemistry 163
chocolate 161
classical 161
climate 155
conference 155
consist 155
contrary 155
couch 155
court 158
credit 161
date 155
deserve 163
details 161
difference 156
economics 158
Ecuador 161
effort 163
employ 163
European 155
everybody 157
everything 161
except 155
experience 163
famous 155

favorite 152
fence 163
fourteenth 162
furnish 163
Garcia 155
grandmother 163
Greek 159
high school 163
hot dog 159
insist 155
interested 155
juice 156
Labor Day 162
Latin 159
law 158
least 155
manners 155
medical 161
melt 163
memorize 158
national 160
opportunity 155
pail 155
Peru 162
pint 155
plenty 155
police 161
Portuguese 152
position 158
post office 161
practical 160
proverb 156
rapidly 163
record 163
Russian 159
salary 158
section 160
shortly 162

simple 160
slippery 155
solution 160
sound 156
speech 155
sport 152
spot 155
stamp 161
statement 155
statue 158
still 152
strict 160
subject 155
substitute 155
supplies 161
suspicious 155
symphony 158
tennis 156
terrible 162
textbook 161
thin 155
unusual 160
ventilation 156
violin 159
war 163
wedding 155
world 155
the World Series 159
worry 155

Let's see now, what does that word mean?

164

LESSON FIFTEEN

15A Word order: words before nouns

1	articles and demonstratives	a, an, the, this, that, etc.
2	possessive words	my, your, John's, etc.
3	ordinal numbers	first, second, next, last, etc.
4	cardinal numbers, words of quantity	one, two, many, few, etc.
5	general description, quality, or character	good, pretty, interesting, etc.
6	size, height, length	little, big, long, tall, etc.
7	age, temperature	new, young, hot, warm, etc.
8	shape	round, square, etc.
9	color, origin, location	red, American, suburban, etc.
10	nouns as adjectives	stone wall, television station

Examples:

(1) the (5) very pretty (6) little (9) Spanish (n) girl

(1) that (2) man's (3) first (4) three (n) children

(4) many (5) important (7) new (10) radio (n) stations

(2) our (3) first (5) good (10) summer (n) weather

(4) very many (5) interesting (7) old (n) houses

(2) Tom's (3) last (6) very big (9) European (n) car

Note: The word very precedes words in groups five to nine and the words many and few in group four.

15B Word order: the word enough

The word enough follows adjectives. However, enough generally precedes nouns.

We have enough time.   It's certainly hot enough now.
There are enough chairs.   That's good enough for now.

165

15C   Word order: the words *something, anything,* etc.

Adjectives follow compound words with <u>every-</u>, <u>some-</u>, <u>any-</u>, and <u>no-</u>, such as <u>something</u>, <u>someone</u>, <u>somebody</u>, <u>anything</u>, etc.

It is <u>something good</u>.   Do you have <u>anything valuable</u>?
<u>Someone else</u> will do it.   <u>Everything bad</u> happened to us.

15D   Word order: measurements

The words <u>wide</u>, <u>old</u>, <u>tall</u>, etc. follow general or specific measurements.

The dog is <u>two years old</u>.   Mr. Brown is <u>six feet tall</u>.
The table is <u>five feet wide</u>.   The baby cried <u>all day long</u>.

15E   Word order: objects, place, manner, and time

	objects		place	manner	time
She went			to a concert	with me	last week.
I will be			at school	for an hour	today.
I know	her			very well	
He likes	candy			very much	
He was			there	for a while	yesterday.
I drove	my car		to Mexico		last year.
We gave	it	to her	at the party		yesterday.
We gave	her	the box	at the party		yesterday.
I studied	the words		in the book	carefully	last night.
He ate	lunch		at home	with us	yesterday.

The normal order of words after verbs is (1) objects, (2) place, (3) manner, and (4) time. The word "manner" includes method, degree, accompaniment, and duration.

Note: English speakers sometimes put the time expression at the beginning of a sentence for emphasis. Idioms such as <u>in general</u>, <u>as usual</u>, etc. frequently occur at the beginning of a sentence.

Review the word order of frequency words, such as <u>always</u>, <u>usually</u>, <u>often</u>, etc. (page 48). Also review the word order of the words <u>already</u>, <u>yet</u>, <u>still</u>, <u>any more</u> (page 153), and the words <u>also</u>, <u>too</u>, etc. (page 154).

15F Strong exclamations with *what* and *how*

The short form of these exclamations does not need a verb.

Short form:	What a story!	How beautiful!
	What nice flowers!	How very pretty!

Full form:

Statement:		This is	a good party.
Exclamation:	What a good party	this is!	

Statement:		She is	very pretty.
Exclamation:	How very pretty	she is!	

15G Words with allied prepositions (part three)

according to: That is wrong according to our instructor.

alongside of: The Central Bank is alongside of the theater.

argue about: The students argued about the new expression.

argue with: Did Charles argue with the students about that?

combine... with: He's going to combine his results with mine.

compare...to: Mr. Brown compared it to the other example. (The two examples are similar.)

compare... with: Mr. Brown compared it with the other example. (He showed us the differences.)

compensate for: Our vacation compensated for a year of hard work. Our pleasure compensated for the expense.

complain about: He frequently complained about the weather.

complain to: They complained to the boss about the trouble.

decide on: Have you decided on a name for your baby yet?

dream about: I didn't dream about anything at all last night.

excited about: They are very excited about the good news.

glance at: Mr. Williams glanced at his wrist watch quickly.

introduce...to: We introduced the students to Mr. Brown.

167

keep an eye on: He kept an eye on our house during our vacation last summer.

live on: They are living on a very small income right now.

loan...to: Smith loaned the money to us about a week ago.

look forward to: They are looking forward to their vacation.

lose faith in: They have lost faith in our ability completely.

mad about: They were quite mad about Betty's sharp reply.

mad at: I'm not mad at her for that. She's mad at them.

make up for: His good pay makes up for his very bad hours.

make use of: We're going to make use of his help very soon.

object to: We objected to his argument. I don't object to it.

pay a compliment to: They paid a nice compliment to him.

pleased with: She was very pleased with her birthday gift.

polite to: The children were very polite to their grandfather.

prepared for: Yes, I'm prepared for the next examination.

proud of: The Wilsons are very proud of their new house.

put a stop to: Please put a stop to that noise immediately!

put a limit on: They've put a limit on the number of guests.

ready for: Are the students ready for the examination yet?

recover from: Has Charles recovered from his injury yet?

rely on: They will probably rely on us for some assistance.

result in: His application resulted in an interview and a job.

satisfied with: He is quite satisfied with the results so far.

spend time on: Don't spend too much time on that question.

take advantage of: Why don't you take advantage of his offer?

take an interest in: He always takes an interest in our work.

take a chance on: Don't take a chance on that. It's not safe.

work for: They work for a very large company in Chicago.

work on: He's working on the tenth chapter of his new book.

Exercise 199   Add the indicated words to the following sentence in the correct word order.

1   <u>blue</u>, <u>large</u>, <u>very</u>, <u>the</u>
He put ____*the very large blue*____ book on the table.

2   <u>wool</u>, <u>pretty</u>, <u>her</u>, <u>new</u>, <u>very</u>
Mary wore _____dress to the party.

3   <u>new</u>, <u>an</u>, <u>historical</u>, <u>interesting</u>
Mr. Smith read _____novel last week.

4   <u>two</u>, <u>those</u>, <u>small</u>, <u>first</u>
_____papers are mine.

5   <u>good looking</u>, <u>his</u>, <u>gabardine</u>, <u>new</u>
John bought _____ suit at that store.

6   <u>hot</u>, <u>some</u>, <u>good</u>, <u>very</u>
We drank_____coffee at the cafeteria.

7   <u>European</u>, <u>an</u>, <u>old</u>, <u>interesting</u>
That is _____custom of theirs.

8   <u>pretty</u>, <u>colonial</u>, <u>new</u>, <u>that</u>, <u>little</u>
We looked at _____house on First Street.

9   <u>comfortable</u>, <u>their</u>, <u>brown</u>, <u>old</u>
They sold _____ chair yesterday.

10   <u>beautiful</u>, <u>Italian</u>, <u>a</u>, <u>new</u>
Mr. Brown has_____ car now.

11   <u>cold</u>, <u>delicious</u>, <u>some</u>, <u>very</u>
We ate _____fruit at lunch.

12   <u>valuable</u>, <u>some</u>, <u>very</u>, <u>old</u>, <u>Roman</u>
The museum owns_____statues.

Exercise 200 Add the indicated words to the following sentence in the correct word order.

1   two, difficult, history, very
    We are studying *two very difficult history* books now.

2   old, lovely, Catholic, a
    There is _____ church in the next block.

3   chilly, a, autumn, very
    Yesterday was _____ day.

4   last, Edward's, two
    _____ names are Garcia and Perez.

5   American, some, boys', two, first
    _____ names are also family names.

6   steel, strong, gray, a
    The machine has _____ cover.

7   tiny, two, flat
    They selected _____ pieces of metal.

8   new, important, federal, an
    That's _____ law.

9   plastic, loose, the
    _____ ring protects it.

10 summer, his, favorite
    _____ sport is golf.

11 gold, delicate, new, a
    She has _____ watch.

12 soft, a, square, rubber
    We bought _____ toy for the dog.

13 unusual, modern, blond, much
    There is _____ furniture in that room.

Exercise 201 Add the indicated expressions to the following sentence in the correct order.

1   last night, to the concert
    We went _to the concert last night_____.

2   tomorrow, at work
    Mr. Williams will be _____.

3   with her father, yesterday, to school
    Miss Smith rode _____.

4   now, carefully

    The student is pronouncing the word _____.

5   for three weeks, in Mexico, next summer
    Mr. and Mrs. Brown will be _____.

6   at the university, this year
    Mr. Gregory is a student _____.

7   every night, very much, at home
    Dick studies _____.

8   on time, every day, to class
    That student comes _____.

9   now, very well
    I know the irregular verbs _____.

10 with his friend, for two hours, at the library
    George is going to study _____.

11 before three, at your house
    We'll arrive _____.

12 now, in the dormitory
    Does he live _____?

13 yesterday, with them, at the lecture
    Were you _____?

Exercise 202 Add the indicated expressions to the following sentence in the correct order.

1 very much, last night
   We liked the movie *very much last night*   .

2 with the boys, to the baseball game, every Sunday
   Mr. Brown goes _____.

3 right now, very hard
   The boys are studying _____.

4 with her grandmother, every summer, to Vermont
   She goes _____.

5 on Thursday, at Wilson's house, by accident
   They met him _____.

6 quickly, a minute ago, down the street
   The boys ran _____.

7 by special delivery, this morning, to us
   Their letter came _____.

8 in Miami, last Tuesday, with his friend
   He arrived _____.

9 carefully, on page 171, last night
   We studied the lesson _____.

10 last year, to England, by plane
    The Wilsons flew _____.

11 about that, recently, to her
    Have you spoken _____?

12 last week, in my head
    I had a bad cold _____.

13 alone, on Saturday, at home
    He did the work _____.

172

Exercise 203   Rewrite the following sentences.   Put the words or expressions in the correct order. Do not change, add, or eliminate any words

1   She - loses - at school - pens - often
              She often loses pens at school.
2   Tom - the show - liked - last night - very much
3   He - knows - now - very well - the irregular verbs
4   They - study - at home - their lessons - in the evening
5   The Browns - have - been - in Ecuador - never
6   That girl - on time - comes - always - to work
7   He - his paycheck - spends - very quickly - usually
8   Bill - is - at the university - this year - a student
9   She - chose - without difficulty - a dress - there
10 He - has - described - to me - them - carefully - never
11 We - sat - until late - with them - in the library - often
12 They - wrote - quickly - the words - on their papers
13 He - explains - always - the lesson - to them - first
14 The boy's - are waiting - friends - three - now - outside
15 He - embarrassed - at the meeting - accidentally - me
16 Someone - took - else - off the table - that glass
17 The table - long - wide - is - six feet - and - 38 inches
18 She - in the kitchen - works - sometimes - for hours
19 He - brings - after work - to his wife - flowers - often
20 She - tells - the news - me - before class - always
21 The water - is - in the pan - now - enough - hot
22 Dick - has - a question - seldom - asked - in class
23 Tom's - is - car - new - high - five feet
24 I - study - over the weekend - seldom - my lessons
25 Don't - speak - you - with your friends - English - ever

Exercise 204 Add the indicated phrases to the following sentence in the correct position.

1   next to ours, from Chicago

The man bought the house. *The man from Chicago bought the house next to ours.*

2   for old people, on the hill

The building is a hospital. _____

3   with red hair, with the red cover

A boy took the book. _____

4   on the table, of that bowl

The shape is interesting. _____

5   on the left, of Mr. Brown's

The man is a friend. _____

6   across the street, of the building

The front is very impressive. _____

7   of meat, of his

That friend bought a pound. _____

8   with Tom, of the pictures

The man took the best one. _____

9   on our west coast, of the ocean

The name is the Pacific. _____

10   on the table, about the war

That book is a good book. _____

11   with the big collar, with the handle

The purse and the coat are mine. _____

12   of Texas, of 267,339 square miles

The state has a land area. _____

13   from Italy, with the white frame

The man took the picture. _____

Exercise 205 Add the indicated words or phrases to the to the following sentence in the correct position.

1 for a light coat, today, enough
   Is it warm? _Is it warm enough for a light coat today?_

2 of that state, of the capital
   What is the name? _____

3 with his friend, still, from Texas, at the library
   Is Dick studying? _____

4 at that store, expensive, with a good lens
   He bought a camera. _____

5 brown, large, old, next to ours
   That house is Mr. Brown's. _____

6 yet, about Jefferson, of that book
   I haven't forgotten the name. _____

7 silver, genuine, for her birthday, to her
   They sent a bracelet. _____

8 too, too, this morning, with my breakfast
   I drank much coffee. _____

9 tomorrow, already, at his house, for the party
   We've bought a cake. _____

10 dinner, from Cuba, after the meeting, at that place
    The doctor ate with them. _____

11 brown, peculiar, only in the winter, of the country
    That bird lives in this section. _____

12 usually, else, to you, besides that
    Does he mention anything? _____

13 either, has he, of that class, to you
    The teacher hasn't spoken about it. _____

Exercise 206 Make strong exclamations with <u>what</u> or <u>how</u>.

1 ____ pretty!
2 ____ a song!
3 ____ a fine morning!
4 ____ easy!
5 ____ a sight!
6 ____ interesting!
7 ____ a good story!
8 ____ exciting!
9 ____ good work!
10 ____ fine features!

what
how

11 ____ beautiful!
12 ____ a hard test!
13 ____ a building!
14 ____ thin!
15 ____ nice people!
16 ____ an easy lesson.
17 ____ ornate!
18 ____ a language!
19 ____ terrible!
20 ____ people!

Exercise 207 Select the correct word from the parentheses.

1 She wore (a, an) old dress yesterday. _____
2 They spoke about (our, ours) friends. _____
3 There are (no, not) any guests in that room. _____
4 (What, Why) did they close the door for? _____
5 (This, These) books belong (to, at, for) her. _____
6 Don't you (ever, never) go (to, in) concerts? _____
7 (Which, What) is your native language? _____
8 They visited (to, two, too) large museums. _____
9 We met (many, much) people last night. _____
10 (It, There) wasn't enough food (on, at) the table. _____
11 (It, There) isn't (enough warm, warm enough). _____
12 They haven't finished it (yet, already). _____
13 We haven't seen them (for, since) five weeks. _____
14 Hasn't he (do, did, done) it (still, yet)? _____
15 My friend sent (me, to me) a nice gift. _____
16 I'll see you a week (from, after) tomorrow. _____
17 Yes, she (is, has) got a lot of them now. _____
18 Did you find (your, yours) books easily? _____
19 That chair is (too, too much) big, isn't it? _____
20 Mr. Brown lives (in, on, at) 652 Park Street. _____
21 He doesn't have (some, any) money with him. _____
22 How (many, much) does the book cost? _____
23 I'm going to study. They are (too, either). _____
24 (What, How) do you call that in English? _____
25 Did you take (one, any) medicine yesterday? _____
26 (Whose, Who's) coats are (this, these)? _____
27 My dress and (her, hers) are quite similar. _____
28 (What, How) a wonderful day this is! _____

29 He doesn't like classical music (also, either) _____
30 (What, How) do (one, you) work this machine? _____
31 She's (falling, fallen) on these steps twice. _____
32 They have written a letter to him (yet, already). _____
33 He isn't going (to, at) school (still, any more). _____
34 I have lived here (for, since) the last war. _____
35 Are (this, these) your photographs? _____
36 (No, Not) many students here speak German. _____
37 George (ever, never) studies at the library. _____
38 I put (to, two, too) much sugar in my coffee. _____
39 (What, How) very pretty that girl is! _____
40 He's (eating, eaten) his dinner right now. _____
41 That furniture (has, have) been here since then. _____
42 How (long, far) is it to Ohio from here? _____
43 I wasn't (in, at) class (last, yesterday) afternoon. _____
44 She wore (a, an) orange dress to the party. _____
45 Is that doctor a friend of (you, your, yours)? _____
46 Does he (yet, still) work at the same place? _____
47 We stayed in Miami (for, since) a month. _____
48 She's (taking, taken) the test twice already. _____
49 (No, Not) many people do it (also, either). _____
50 What city is New York University (in, on, at)? _____
51 Is that your book or (our, ours)? _____
52 They ate (some, any) ice cream for dessert. _____
53 The building is (in, on, at) 116th Street. _____
54 Charles gave (me, to me) the money yesterday. _____
55 (This, These) are very pretty flowers. _____
56 (No, Not) members did it, (did, didn't) they? _____
57 He's (knowing, known) that (in, for) a long time. _____
58 Has John returned from downtown (yet, still)? _____
59 (It, There) was a big party here last night. _____
60 (It, There) was a fine day yesterday. _____
61 Mr. Wilson (too, also) enjoys poker and bridge. _____
62 It doesn't (very, quite) often rain in this section. _____
63 The Browns don't (often, seldom) do that. _____
64 (Why, What) about that? Isn't it right? _____
65 Isn't there (several, any) time for that now? _____
66 (Why, What) did he say that to them? _____
67 Hasn't it been there (several, any) times before? _____
68 (Why, What) did they mention it to him for? _____

Exercise 208 Use the <u>past tense</u> or the <u>present perfect</u> <u>tense</u> of each verb.

I finished it a short time ago.

1 I (finish) it a short time ago. _____
2 Dick ____not (quit) his job yet. _____
3 He (study) Russian before the last war. _____
4 We (have) very little trouble with it so far. _____
5 They (be) in Moscow until two months ago. _____
6 Up to now, she (make) good progress. _____
7 Formerly, we (work) in the same factory. _____
8 We (drive) ninety miles this morning. _____
9 The telegram (arrive) just a minute ago. _____
10 ____you ever (visit) the Soviet Union? _____
11 Yes, we (be) there from 1947 to 1949. _____
12 I (understand, never) those instructions. _____
13 Maybe George (leave) before seven o'clock. ____
14 We ____not (hear) from him for a long time. ____
15 Thus far, they (do, always) that for us. _____
16 He (work) here for the past three weeks. _____
17 She (finish, finally) that hard exercise! _____
18 Up to the present, I (believe, always) them. ____
19 Before her graduation, she (apply) for a job. ____
20 We (hear) some bad news a little while ago. ____
21 I (send, already) a special delivery letter. ____
22 ____you (get) to Spain during your trip? _____
23 Yes. In fact, we (go) there twice on the trip. ____
24 ____you (write) to your friends since then? ____
25 We ____not (hear) from Betty and Pat yet. ____

Exercise 209 Use <u>since</u>, <u>for</u>, <u>until</u>, or <u>by</u>.

1 They'll be ready for us _____noon.   _____
2 We were there _____eight o'clock last night.   _____
3 I've been here ____the beginning of the semester.   _____
4 ____two days ago, I thought so too.   _____
5 They were here _____two or three years.   _____
6 I won't be back ____later this afternoon.   _____
7 Everything will be ready for you ____then.   _____
8 They were in Italy _____1940.   _____
9 Then they went to Brazil ____a year or two.   _____
10 They'll know all about it ____that time.   _____
11 She has never agreed with us _____now.   _____
12 He has never mentioned it ____the election.   _____
13 He probably won't do it ____the next election.   _____

178

Exercise 210 Supply the correct prepositions.

1 He's excited ____ his new job.
2 Are you ready ____ the guests yet?
3 They argued ____ us ____ it last night.
4 He was quite pleased ____ the results.
5 Williams is working ____ an export company.
6 Don't worry ____ it. Everything will be here.
7 Did you call his attention ____ their mistake?
8 He was proud ____ his mark ____ the examination.
9 The bookcase is right next ____ the fireplace.
10 He takes a lot of interest ____ our work.
11 We are quite prepared ____ their arguments.
12 How do you live ____ thirty dollars a week?
13 Is Miss Wilson very fond ____ French food?
14 Yes. ____ fact, I'm interested ____ that too.
15 I insisted ____ a prompt reply ____ my request.
16 Why is Charles so mad ____ them?
17 When are they leaving ____ the west coast?
18 They're going to take a chance ____ that.
19 He depends ____ his sister ____ assistance.
20 We're very sorry ____ our mistake.
21 I glanced ____ the advertisement briefly.
22 What did you dream ____ last night?
23 According ____ Bill, there's something wrong.
24 They arrived ____ the train station late.
25 He worked ____ his lessons ____ half an hour.
26 She's afraid ____ cats ____ some reason or other.
27 I'm still not accustomed ____ this weather.
28 He put a stop ____ that very quickly.
29 I'll introduce you ____ them ____ a minute or two.
30 Except ____ that one, the sentences were easy.
31 They complained ____ the teacher ____ the lesson.
32 We didn't care ____ the movie ____ all!
33 Be careful! They'll lose faith ____ you.
34 I'm going to borrow a book ____ them ____ you.
35 They were very polite ____ us ____ the meeting.
36 I paid thirty-eight dollars ____ that bracelet.
37 I'm quite certain ____ the price ____ it.
38 Please make use ____ it if ____ all possible.
39 Are you very familiar ____ that method?
40 ____ whom do these English books belong?

179

VOCABULARY FOR LESSON FIFTEEN

Pages 165 - 179

accidentally 173
ability 168
according 168
alongside 168
apply 178
area 174
argue 168
autumn 170
believe 178
besides 175
bird 175
blond 170
bookcase 179
bowl 174
briefly 179
candidate 179
capital 175
Catholic 170
chilly 170
coast 174
collar 174
colonial 169
compare 167
compensate 167
complain 168
completely 168
dormitory 171
dream 168
easily 176
embarrass 173
excited 168
exciting 176
export 174
federal 170
fine 176
fireplace 179
flat 170
formerly 178

frame 174
gabardine 169
genuine 175
glance 168
gold 169
golf 170
graduation 178
grandfather 168
grandmother 172
handle 174
head 172
impressive 174
interview 168
Jefferson 175
lens 175
loan 168
loose 170
lovely 170
mark 179
metal 170
method 179
modern 170
Moscow 178
native language 176
object 168
ocean 174
ornate 176
the Pacific 174
paycheck 173
peculiar 175
plastic 170
pleased 168
pleasure 168
polite 168
poker 177
possible 179
prepared 168
prompt 179

protect 170
proud 168
recently 172
recover 168
rely 168
request 179
result 168
ring 170
rubber 170
safe 168
satisfied 168
select 170
shape 174
sight 176
silver 175
soft 170
the Soviet Union 178
square 165
steel 170
stone 165
suburban 165
tiny 170
Vermont 172
valuable 165
west 179
without 173
wool 169

I know all of these words. How about you?

180

LESSON SIXTEEN

16A   The comparative and superlative forms

In English, adjectives sometimes have different forms for comparisons. Notice the difference between type [1] and type [2].

Type [1] Words of one syllable and words of two syllables with -y, -ow, or -er at the end.

tall	taller	the tallest
pretty	prettier	the prettiest

Type [2] Words of two or more syllables.

intelligent	more intelligent less intelligent	the most intelligent the least intelligent

COMPARISON OF TWO THINGS:

John is		taller		than	Tom.
John is	the	taller		of	the two boys.
John has	a	bigger	car	than	he.
John has		bigger	hands	than	Tom.

John is		more intelligent		than	Tom.
John is	the	more intelligent		of	the two boys.
John has	a	more important	job	than	he.
John has		more important	friends	than	Tom.

Notice the use of (1) an adjective of comparison + than or (2) an adjective of comparison + a noun + than.

Examples:
  Mr. Johnson's new car is smaller than yours.
  That brown chair is more comfortable than this one.
  That man is much more polite than his friend is.
  Mr. Smith has much more money than Mr. Johnson.
  Mr. Johnson has many more books than Mr. Smith.
  There are more students in that class than in this one.
  More students in this school study Spanish than Chinese.

ONE FROM THREE OR MORE THINGS:

George is	the biggest		of	the three boys.
George is	the biggest	boy	of in	all. the class.

George is	the most intelligent		of	the three boys.
George is	the most intelligent	boy	of in	all. the class.

Note: The word <u>boy</u> in the preceding sentences is optional.

Examples:

The tallest person in our office is Frank.
The heaviest box of all is that big one.
That chair is the most comfortable one in the house.
That is the most difficult of all the chapters so far.

16B Spelling the comparative and superlative forms

[1]

[2] final -e

[3] final -y

[4] one vowel + one
final consonant

short smart	shorter smarter	shortest smartest
wise cute	wiser cuter	wisest cutest
funny pretty	funnier prettier	funniest prettiest
fat thin	fatter thinner	fattest thinnest

16C Words with irregular comparatives and superlatives

bad	worse	worst
far	farther further	farthest furthest
good	better	best

little	less	least
much many	more	most

16D Comparisons with *as ... as*

That student	is	as	tall intelligent	as	his sister is.
That student	isn't	as	tall intelligent	as	she.

Note: In negative sentences, <u>so...as</u> is also correct.
Notice the special expressions <u>as much</u> and <u>as many</u>. Also
review section 5 D on page 46.

Mr. Wilson has	as much money as	Mr. Johnson.
Mr. Wilson has	as many friends as	Mr. Johnson.

There are very many proverbial expressions with <u>as...as</u>.

as red as a beet   as smart as a fox
as pretty as a picture   as quiet as a mouse

16E General comparisons

Type [1]

Your new table is	the same	as	my table.
Your new table is	like		mine.
Your new table is	similar	to	my table.
Your new table is	different	from	mine.

Type [2]

That new table and	my table	are	the same.
That new table and	mine	are	alike.
That new table and	my table	are	similar.
That new table and	yours	are	different.

16F The words *same* and *different* with nouns

Your new spring coat is	the same	color	as	mine.
Your new spring coat is	a different	color	from	mine.

Note: Native speakers of English also use the expression
<u>different...than</u> quite commonly.

16G The expression *one of* with the superlative

Study the following sentences carefully. Note: a plural
noun follows the superlative form of the adjective.

Paris is	one of	the prettiest	cities	in the world.
Mary is	one of	the most beautiful	girls	in the school.

16H   Idioms

as a (general) rule: As a general rule, I finish quite early.

as a matter of fact: Of course he will help you. As a matter of fact, he'll probably do all of the work for you.

as a result of: As a result of the rain yesterday, I didn't go.

as before: As before, we'll return everything to your office.

as soon as possible: Please finish that as soon as possible.

as usual: As usual, he wants more than everyone else here.

at best: At best, he will get only an average grade on this.

at least: The thief stole my jewelry.   -- Well, at least he didn't take your money too.

at one's worst: He was at his worst during the tournament.

at (the) most: At most, we'll lose only five or ten minutes.

because of: We didn't go to his house because of the weather.

(the) best of all: Elizabeth likes that dress the best of all.

better than ever: He's doing better than ever in his business.

do one's best: Please do your best work on this project.

first of all: First of all, there are several important items.

for that reason: For that reason, we're not going to try it.

for the best: Everything probably happened for the best.

for the most part: We agree with them for the most part.

instead of: She bought the red dress instead of the blue one.

in the least: They didn't care for that movie in the least.

make the best of: They made the best of a difficult situation.

more or less: Is that answer right? -- Yes, more or less.

more than ever: More students than ever are learning English. How does he like it now? -- More than ever.

once more: Dick's going to try the same thing once more.

sooner or later: He will have an accident sooner or later.

Exercise 211 Write the comparative and superlative forms of the following adjectives.

Words like these have three forms.

1	fast *faster the fastest*	11	smart ___ ___
2	wide ___ ___	12	long ___ ___
3	large ___ ___	13	tall ___ ___
4	deep ___ ___	14	short ___ ___
5	busy ___ ___	15	slow ___ ___
6	thin ___ ___	16	heavy ___ ___
7	pretty ___ ___	17	young ___ ___
8	fat ___ ___	18	funny ___ ___
9	cute ___ ___	19	old ___ ___
10	big ___ ___	20	small ___ ___

Exercise 212 Make comparisons with the adjectives given in the sentences.

1 I am (big) he. ___ *I am bigger than he.*
2 Tom is (small) his brother. ___
3 This house is (expensive) that one. ___
4 However, this one is (old) that one. ___
5 This car is (good) the other one. ___
6 The other car is much (bad) this one. ___
7 Charles is always (serious) Tom. ___
8 Dick is usually (thoughtful) Harry. ___
9 This cloth is much (dry) yours is. ___
10 Her bracelet is (valuable) mine. ___
11 Betty is a great deal (beautiful) her friend. ___
12 Their office was (busy) our office. ___
13 The weather is (warm) today ___ yesterday. ___
14 That city is (far) from here ___ Miami. ___
15 (Many) students study Spanish ___ German. ___
16 Boston is (close) to New York ___ Chicago. ___
17 Dick is a (ambitious) student ___ Charles. ___
18 Charles has (many) friends ___ Bill. ___
19 They have (expensive) furniture ___ we. ___
20 My brother has (much) money ___ I. ___
21 He's a much (homely) boy ___ John. ___
22 (Few) members came this year ___ last year. ___
23 We got much (good) results ___ that. ___

Exercise 213 Make comparisons with <u>as...as</u>.

1 I am (tall) Dick. _____ *I am as tall as Dick*.
2 Bill is (polite) his brother. _____
3 Tom isn't (heavy) Bill is. _____
4 She is (popular) her sister. _____
5 That table isn't (narrow) this one. _____
6 This room is (wide) the other one. _____
7 This exercise is (easy) the last one. _____
8 This fruit isn't (sweet) that. _____
9 That novel is (good) this one. _____
10 The tall girl is (pretty) the dark one. _____
11 She's not quite (nervous) her brother. _____
12 Bill is (serious) a student ___ Charles. _____
13 Smith has (much) money ___ Jones. _____
14 They have (many) books ___ we. _____
15 That city has (narrow) streets ___ this city. _____
16 Does your country have (bad) weather ___ this? _____
17 He isn't (brilliant) a man ___ his father. _____
18 I'm not (energetic) a person ___ Brown. _____

Exercise 214 Use the superlative form of the adjective given in each sentence.

That's the oldest chair of all.

1 That's (old) chair of all. _____
2 This is (big) room in the building. _____
3 Tom is (reserved) boy in this class. _____
4 Bill is (bright) student of all. _____
5 Betty is (friendly) girl in this office. _____
6 This is (attractive) room in the whole house. _____
7 Charles writes (good) papers of all. _____
8 This is (bad) weather so far this year. _____
9 That's (comfortable) chair in this room. _____
10 John has (little) talent of anyone in the group. _____
11 She's (thoughtful) one in that family. _____
12 New York has (many) tall buildings of any city. _____
13 Brazil exports (much) coffee of all countries. _____
14 That brown house costs (little) of the three. _____
15 That last lesson was (good) of all. _____
16 That man is (conceited) in our office. _____
17 This small table is (new) in the house. _____
18 He was (sensible) one at the meeting by far. _____
19 That last exercise was (complicated) of all so far. _____
20 George is (clumsy) of the four players. _____

Exercise 215 Complete these sentences with the following words: <u>than</u>, <u>as</u>, <u>of</u>, <u>from</u>, or <u>in</u>.

1 This table is as big____that one.
2 The red book is bigger____the blue one.
3 John is the best student____the class.
4 This book is more interesting____that one.
5 This one is the largest____all the apples.
6 This exercise is different____the last one.
7 Charles is the same size____the older boy.
8 Charles is larger _____ the other two boys.
9 Charles is the larger _____ the two.
10 Charles is the largest _____ all the boys.
11 That car is the same kind _____ this one.
12 These seats aren't as comfortable ____those.
13 This one is the prettiest ____all.
14 He's the most intelligent man____ the organization.
15 This one is a little less difficult ____the other one.

Exercise 216 Use the adjectives in the sentences correctly.

1 That's (easy) of all. _____*That's the easiest of all.*
2 It's (big) than Bill's. _____*It's bigger than Bill's.*
3 He's (rude) man in the group. _____
4 John is (tactful) than his brother. _____
5 This book is (exciting) than that one. _____
6 That coat is (same) as mine. _____
7 Is this book (good) than that one? _____
8 He's (stupid) boy in the class. _____
9 Dick's (polite) than the other fellow. _____
10 That house isn't (new) as Mr. Brown's. _____
11 Is Charles (young) than his sister? _____
12 Our books are (different) yours. _____
13 He is (popular) fellow in the club. _____
14 Is Helen (charming) as her sister? _____
15 Detroit is (far) from here than Boston. _____
16 That picture is quite (similar) this one. _____
17 This cartoon is (funny) than that one. _____
18 That paper is (smooth) of all the types. _____
19 She has (little) difficulty with this than that. _____
20 This piece of wood is (thick) as those two. _____
21 That seems much (normal) than the other. _____
22 Are there (many) people there than here? _____
23 Mary's (pretty) as the tall dark girl. _____

187

Exercise 217 Compare Tom and Dick. Use the comparative forms of the indicated words.

TOM   DICK   HARRY

neat	rich
big	smart
heavy	lazy
funny	selfish
formal	small
sociable	old
foolish	reserved
ambitious	busy
young	considerate
popular	respectful
polite	confident
intelligent	thoughtful

Exercise 218 Compare Tom, Dick, and Harry. Use the superlative forms of the indicated words.

fat	thin	large	weak
lonely	strange	dark	calm
careful	helpful	patient	sincere
curious	generous	liberal	awkward

Exercise 219 Compare Charles Johnson's house and Mr. Brown's house. For example, compare these things:

the sizes (big, small, etc.)
the prices (cheap, expensive, etc.)
the number of people in each house
the number of windows in each house

JOHNSON'S HOUSE BROWN'S HOUSE   WILSON'S HOUSE

Exercise 220 Use superlative forms for the three houses.

Exercise 221 Select the correct word for each sentence.

1 He was there (in, for, since) three or four years.
2 He's been at the university (in, until, since) 1950.
3 I married my sweetheart (in, since, during) the war.
4 The plane is leaving (in, by, for) fifteen minutes.
5 He was here (for, since, until) late in the evening.
6 She'll stay there from June (by, for, until) August.
7 Dick will remain here (by, for, until) ten-thirty.
8 We'll leave (in, on, from) the middle of the lecture.
9 I'm going to study it (to, by, for) the next ten months.
10 We've been in this country (at, from, since) last June.
11 We went there twice (by, since, during) the summer.
12 Smith will be back (in, by, during) a few minutes.
13 I drove my car (in, for, during) two hours yesterday.
14 They'll finish the job (to, by, at) next November.
15 He'll visit the Louvre (at, until, during) his vacation.
16 She's been here (by, from, since) the first of July.
17 We stayed at the meeting (at, by, until) 12:30 p.m.
18 He'll be here from April 19 (at, on, until) August 21.
19 Bill was absent (for, from, since) two days last week.
20 He became sick (at, to, since) the party last Friday.
21 The men will return (in, by, until) half an hour or so.
22 We've known Mr. Smith (by, for, since) many years.
23 They returned from Cuba late (in, on, at) the spring.
24 I've done that (by, for, since) more than five years.
25 Mr. Williams was born (in, on, at) the year 1910.
26 We're going to meet them (in, on, at) Thursday.
27 His last letter arrived here (in, on, at) October 17.
28 They'll be back here (in, to, from) an hour or so.
29 Brown will be away (in, for, until) several months.
30 Mr. White has lived there (from, since, until) 1948.
31 He's taught here (for, from, since) ten years now.
32 The dinner won't be ready (to, for, until) six-thirty.
33 The dinner lasted (to, for, since) an hour and a half.
34 We've done 16 lessons (from, until, since) October.
35 Didn't Brown get a letter (to, at, for) that time?
36 She's going (in, to, during) her Christmas vacation.
37 Won't those packages be ready (in, at, until) then?
38 The agent waited for him (in, by, until) last month.
39 The movie will be over (in, by, for) a half an hour.
40 Will you help me (for, until, during) a few minutes?

Exercise 222 Add the indicated word or words to each sentence. In some instances, there are two possibilities.

(part one)

1 (still) John is here. _____ *John is still here.*
2 (yet) Has Tom finished the job? _____
3 (always) Do you study at home? _____
4 (to us) The professor explained it. _____
5 (already) They have eaten dinner. _____
6 (old) That's an interesting custom. _____
7 (still) Does she work at the library? _____
8 (also) The boys like football. _____
9 (usually) The director is in his office. _____
10 (yet) Do they know the answer? _____
11 (there) They go every weekend. _____
12 (with her) He went to the movies last night. _____
13 (to her) Did you send that big package? _____
14 (already) She has completed the work. _____
15 (either) He doesn't care for classical music. _____

(part two)

16 (still) I don't remember his name. _____
17 (to us) They returned the books yesterday. _____
18 (already) He has sent the letter, hasn't he? _____
19 (always) They don't do good work. _____
20 (red) What pretty hair she has! _____
21 (also) They enjoy popular music. _____
22 (always) Is there someone here? _____
23 (new) We bought a pretty square clock. _____
24 (there) Do you go every summer? _____
25 (yet) You haven't spoken to him, have you? _____
26 (two) The boy's books are over there. _____
27 (too) Mary eats many sweet things. _____
28 (by plane) We went to England last spring. _____
29 (to him) Have you sent the letter or not? _____
30 (still) Are you studying at that school? _____
31 (already) I have seen that movie. _____
32 (either) They don't know about it, do they? _____
33 (never) We have been to that museum. _____
34 (to the concert) I went with him last night. _____
35 (ever) Does Charles eat at the cafeteria? _____

Exercise 223 Use the correct tense of the indicated verb.
(part one)

1 He (need) it right now. _____ *He needs it right now.*
2 I always (eat) one egg for breakfast. _____
3 She (give) the money to me yesterday. _____
4 I (see) that movie twice already. _____
5 He (do) the report an hour from now. _____
6 She (speak) both French and English well. _____
7 They (write) some letters right now. _____
8 The store (have) two big sales since then. _____
9 There (be) many people here tomorrow. _____
10 There (be) two storms in the last three days. _____
11 (Quit) that at once! _____
12 Bill (lend) him some money two weeks ago. _____
13 The news (be) very interesting yesterday. _____
14 Our teacher (teach) in this same school ten years. _____
15 John (take) a course in Spanish last year. _____

(part two)

16 Listen! I (hear) someone at the door. _____
17 He (put) it there a few minutes ago. _____
18 She (come) into the room right now. _____
19 Mrs. Brown (wear) her new suit yesterday. _____
20 They (arrive) a week from Friday. _____
21 She (sing) a song for us in a few minutes. _____
22 George (be) quite sick last weekend. _____
23 Ralph (be) in the hospital since May. _____
24 They (buy) a new car last month. _____
25 I (forget) the name of it already. _____
26 (Shut) the door, please. _____
27 He (send) the letter tomorrow morning. _____
28 We (read) the assignment last night. _____
29 They (tell) me all about that already. _____
30 The United States (be) quite a large country. _____
31 Everything (go) quite well so far. _____
32 Wilson (return) a week from Thursday. _____
33 Up to now, They (have) a very good time. _____
34 I (have) the same car for the last five years. _____
35 We (write) almost every exercise so far. _____
36 I (do) Exercise 223 right now. _____
37 I (finish, finally) this exercise! _____

VOCABULARY FOR LESSON SIXTEEN

Pages 181 - 191

ambitious 185
as 182
attractive 186
average 183
awkward 188
Baton Rouge 191
best 182
better 182
bright 186
brilliant 186
calm 188
cartoon 187
charming 187
clumsy 186
complicated 186
conceited 186
confident 188
considerate 188
curious 188
deep 185
director 190
dry 185
energetic 186
farther 182
farthest 182
fellow 187
foolish 188
formal 188
friendly 186
further 182
furthest 182
generous 188
grade 183
homely 185
item 184
jewelry 183
Jones 186

lazy 188
less 182
liberal 188
marry 189
most 181
narrow 186
neat 188
nervous 186
normal 187
patient 188
person 186
player 186
project 184
reserved 186
respectful 188
rude 187
selfish 188
sensible 186
sincere 188
size 188
slow 185
sociable 188
strange 188
stupid 189
sweet 186
sweetheart 189
tactful 187
thick 187
thoughtful 185
tournament 184
type 187
way 190
whole 186
wood 187
worse 182
worst 182

Well, I've done the next to last lesson. I'm almost through.

LESSON SEVENTEEN

17A The passive forms of verbs

Passive verbs are formed by using the verb be + the third
form of another verb.

he	is	known
he	was	known
he	will be	known
he	has been	known
they	have been	known

Simple present:

Past:

Future:

Present perfect:

The "subject" performs or directs the action of an "active"
verb. The "subject" receives the action of a "passive" verb.

subject	active verb	object	
The teacher	corrects	my lesson	every day.
The teacher	corrects	my lessons	every day.

subject	passive verb	agent	
My lesson	is corrected	by the teacher	every day.
My lessons	are corrected	by the teacher	every day.

A passive verb sometimes occurs without an "agent." In
this case, the "agent" is not important or essential.

Mr. Brown's house <u>was built</u> last summer.
Our mail <u>is</u> always <u>delivered</u> in the morning.

17B Statements, questions, and negatives

	The packages	were		returned	by Tom.
Were	the packages			returned	by Tom?
	The packages	weren't		returned	by Tom.
Weren't	the packages			returned	by Tom?

	The work	will	be	finished	by ten.
Will	the work		be	finished	by ten?
	The work	won't	be	finished	by ten.
Won't	the work		be	finished	by ten?

Notice the position of <u>always</u>, <u>already</u>, and <u>yet</u> in these sentences with passive verbs.

Is	The mail the mail	is	always always	delivered delivered	at this time. at this time?
Isn't	The mail the mail	isn't	always always	delivered delivered	at this time. at this time?

Has	The letter the letter	has	already	been sent. been sent	yet?
Hasn't	The letter the letter	hasn't		been sent been sent	yet. yet?

17C   The infinitive after certain verbs

The infinitive is the basic form of a verb.   The infinitive of the verbs <u>eats</u> and <u>ate</u> is <u>eat</u>. (The infinitive of <u>is</u> and <u>are</u> is <u>be</u>.) <u>To eat</u> is the full infinitive.   <u>To</u> is "the sign of the infinitive." The full infinitive follows certain verbs. Note: the infinitive does not change its form after different tenses or persons (<u>we</u>, <u>you</u>, <u>he</u>, etc.).

He	wants	the candy.	
He	wants	to eat.	
He	wants	to eat	the candy.

I	want	to leave	soon.
He	wants	to leave	soon.
He	wanted	to leave	soon.

The full infinitive is used after these verbs: <u>agree</u>, <u>claim</u>, <u>dare</u>, <u>decide</u>, <u>expect</u>, <u>fail</u>, <u>hope</u>, <u>intend</u>, <u>learn</u>, <u>need</u>, <u>offer</u>, <u>plan</u>, <u>pretend</u>, <u>promise</u>, <u>refuse</u>, <u>resolve</u>, <u>seem</u>, <u>try</u>, <u>want</u>, and <u>wish</u>.

E x a m p l e s :

We expect <u>to return</u> late in the summer.
She hopes <u>to finish</u> the work within an hour.
They learned <u>to understand</u> English quickly.
He plans <u>to leave</u> for Europe on the same boat.

Certain of these verbs (<u>expect</u>, <u>hope</u>, <u>plan</u>) + the full infinitive convey the idea of future action.   However, the verb <u>think</u> is never used for this purpose.

Two infinitives sometimes occur in a sentence successively.

The students wanted	to learn	to speak	English well.

194

17D The infinitive to show purpose

The full infinitive also shows "purpose." In this case, in order to is a substitute for to ("the sign of the infinitive").

Examples:

> I suggested that to help them.
> (or: I suggested that in order to help them.)
> We went to the meeting to hear the news.
> I stood on my toes to see over their heads.
> Charles removed the cover to show it to me.

17E The gerund after certain verbs

The gerund is the "-ing" form of the verb (working, studying, living, etc.). Certain verbs are followed by the gerund, not the full infinitive. Note: the gerund does not change its form after different persons (we, she, etc.) or tenses.

I enjoy	English.	
I enjoy	studying.	
I enjoy	studying	English.

I	avoid	working	hard.
He	avoids	working	hard.
He	avoided	working	hard.

The gerund is used after the following verbs: admit, appreciate, avoid, consider, delay, deny, enjoy, finish, keep on ("continue"), mind, postpone, practice, put off ("postpone"), recall, regret, resent, stop, and suggest.

> Everyone enjoys learning something new.
> Mr. Smith will finish writing letters shortly.
> They have postponed doing that for a while.
> He often practices speaking English with me.

Gerunds are sometimes followed by full infinitives. Likewise, full infinitives are sometimes followed by gerunds. Less often, two gerunds follow one another.

Those people enjoyed	learning	to speak	English.
Mr. Wilson decided	to finish	working	here first.
The women suggested	postponing	doing	the work.

17F   The gerund after prepositions

The gerund, not the infinitive, is used after prepositions.

The students got good marks	by	studying.
She takes a lot of interest	in	helping people.
The three men objected	to	returning so soon.
Mr. Brown is very good	at	remembering names.

17G   The infinitive or gerund after certain verbs

These verbs are followed by either the full infinitive or the gerund without a change in meaning: begin, continue, hate, intend, like, love, prefer, start

Examples:

Many people like to swim in the ocean.
Many people like swimming in the ocean.

When did you begin to study English here?
When did you begin studying English here?

17H   Idioms

be accustomed to: We are accustomed to criticism. I am accustomed to leaving at that time.

be used to: We are used to the weather now. I am used to getting criticism.

by far: Adams is by far the best salesman in the company.

by now: By now, they have probably heard the bad news.

have something to do with: Where does he work? -- I'm not sure, but he has something to do with the university. He didn't have anything to do with our suggestion.

nothing doing: Please help us. -- I'm sorry. Nothing doing.

to be sure ["certainly"]: To be sure, we approve of that.

to say the least: They despised that fellow to say the least.

too good to be true: That news is really too good to be true.

turn off: He turned off the lights ten minutes ago. Please turn off the water for me.

turn on: Please turn on the lights. He turned on the water.

well to do: Is he wealthy? -- Yes, he is very well to do.

Exercise 224   Use only <u>the past tense</u> of each verb.

1   The work (finish) yesterday. _It was finished yesterday._
2   The glasses (break) accidentally. _____
3   The furniture (repair) by the carpenter. _____
4   Jones (make) two suggestions to us. _____
5   The president (elect) in November. _____
6   The news (announce) yesterday. _____
7   The men (do) the entire job for us. _____
8   The money (steal) last night. _____
9   Two people (injure) in the accident. _____
10 The house (sell) for less than $15,000. _____

Exercise 225   Use only <u>the future tense</u> of each verb.

1   You (assist) by them. _You will be assisted by them._
2   The packages (deliver) tomorrow. _____
3   A new man (manage) that store. _____
4   The letters (finish) by that time. _____
5   The grass (ruin) by this hot sun. _____
6   A new house (build) here next year. _____
7   The news (know) by everybody soon. _____
8   You (permit) to leave early today. _____
9   Mr. Brown (teach) our class tomorrow. _____
10 We (delay) two days by the weather. _____

Exercise 226   Use <u>the present perfect tense</u> of each verb.

1   The room (clean). _The room has been cleaned._
2   That (suggest) by them already. _____
3   You (choose) secretary by the members. _____
4   That new house (buy) already. _____
5   We (advise) them to try again. _____
6   The two letters (write) already. _____
7   He (permit) to stay a year longer. _____
8   Three different men (teach) us already. _____
9   The flowers (deliver) to her already. _____
10 The dishes (put) in the cupboard already. _____
11 The order (cancel) by that firm. _____
12 The man in the store (cheat) them. _____
13 That (request, already) by the director. _____
14 So far, only two buildings (construct). _____
15 Everyone (blame) us for the trouble. _____

Exercise 227 Change the verb from active to passive form.
Keep the same tense.

1 He closed the door. _____ *The door was closed by him*.
2 She opens the mail every day. _____
3 Mr. Brown will sign the letter. _____
4 The students enjoyed the lecture. _____
5 She has received the letter already. _____
6 They ate the chocolate candy. _____
7 He always takes care of that. _____
8 Mr. White repaired the car. _____

9 Does the secretary answer the phone? _____
10 Did the boys move the chairs? _____
11 Will he deliver the books to them? _____
12 Has she written the letter? _____
13 Do they admit foreign students? _____
14 Did he mail that big package? _____
15 Have the boys eaten the cake? _____

16 They didn't return the books. _____
17 She doesn't sign the checks. _____
18 He will not move the furniture. _____
19 Didn't he finish the work? _____
20 Won't your lawyer do that? _____

Exercise 228 Change the verb from passive to active form.
Keep the same tense.

1 It was taken by him. _____ *He took it*.
2 They will be delivered by her. _____
3 He wasn't trusted by the other men. _____
4 They were frightened by the loud noise. _____
5 My bracelet has been stolen by somebody. _____
6 Were the papers signed by him? _____
7 The dinner was prepared by the cook. _____
8 The report has been completed by them. _____
9 The fog was blown away by the warm breeze. _____
10 Several books have been borrowed by students. _____
11 The envelope will be returned by the messenger. _____
12 Her dress was made by her grandmother. _____
13 Many things were stolen by the thieves. _____
14 Our exercises are corrected by the teacher. _____
15 Was the whole house painted by the men? _____

Exercise 229 Supply the correct form of the verb in each sentence. Notice the five different forms of a typical verb:

eat, eats, eating, ate, eaten

1   He'll (write) it tomorrow. _He'll write it tomorrow._
2   I suggest (demand) that. _I suggest demanding that._
3   He intends to (go) on a trip. _____
4   Almost everyone enjoys (increase) his knowledge. __
5   We were (permit) to (stay) a month longer. _____
6   Alice has (take) two courses in Russian. _____
7   The two packages were (take) by the messenger. ____
8   He plans to (return) to his country next year. _____
9   Tom usually (try) to (do) careful work. _____
10 I am (look) forward to (do) that sometime soon. ____
11 English is (speak) by a large number of people. _____
12 I prefer to (warn) them before (stop) it. _____
13 We were (bore) by his very long speech. _____
14 Frank usually (have) his lunch with them. _____
15 He admitted (quarrel) with the other officials. _____
16 She decided to (leave) before eight o'clock. _____
17 The project will be (complete) sometime next year. __
18 The children are (behave) very well this evening. ____
19 The men considered (interrupt) the conference. _____
20 That big house has been (sell) already. _____
21 He insisted on (spoil) everything by (criticize) it. __
22 Harry will (come) back in a few minutes. _____
23 We are (study) the infinitives and gerunds now. _____
24 He avoided (join) that organization last year. _____
25 Have you (spend) all of your money already? _____
26 The machinery has been (inspect) by them already. __
27 Many of the machines were (break) by careless men. __
28 When did you finish (repair) the machinery? _____
29 Mrs. Brown (wear) her new coat yesterday. _____
30 He made up for (damage) it by (fix) it. _____
31 Did they (do) all of their part carefully? _____
32 Was their part (do) in time to (help) you? _____
33 They practiced (pronounce) the new words with me. __
34 That has been (do) several times before this. _____
35 She has (do) all of the work very carefully. _____
36 He takes an interest in (discover) new things. _____
37 Bill generally (hurry) to his office in the morning. __
38 They object to (try) to (reduce) the amount. _____

Exercise 230 Use the gerund or the full infinitive form of the indicated verb in each sentence.

1 He plans (leave) soon. _____ *He plans to leave soon.*
2 They enjoyed (hear) the lecture. _____
3 She's doing it (assist) them. _____
4 Bill is good at (learn) new words. _____
5 The man promised (send) it soon. _____
6 We listened carefully (hear) everything. _____
7 Did the other men object to (change) it? _____
8 The Browns hope (buy) a house next year. _____
9 Why don't you suggest (have) it here? _____
10 I learned (be) careful about certain things. _____
11 Tom went to the store (get) some cigarettes. _____
12 We learn English by (practice) it constantly. _____
13 John wishes (become) a doctor or dentist. _____
14 I discussed it with him (get) his ideas about it. _____
15 She expects (hear) from them tomorrow. _____
16 They postponed (do) it until Thursday. _____
17 Their reasons for (do) it weren't clear to us. _____
18 Did your friend consider (travel) by air? _____
19 Do they intend (leave) the country very soon? _____
20 We'll need some help (finish) it soon enough. _____

Exercise 231 Change these statements to questions.

1 It is raining now. _____ *Is it raining now?*
2 He usually studies in the evening. _____
3 My coat is torn on the sleeve. _____
4 They have taken it away already. _____
5 We were advised to try again later. _____
6 There will be some Brazilian men at the meeting. _____
7 We often practice by repeating the sentences. _____
8 He will try to do better next time. _____
9 We haven't seen the pictures yet. _____
10 That plan was also suggested by someone else. _____
11 She promised to return it to us by Tuesday. _____
12 Portuguese is spoken in Brazil. _____
13 Dick knows more than two thousand words. _____
14 He has always enjoyed learning languages. _____
15 They learned to speak Portuguese in one year. _____
16 Tom and Bill drove to Washington together. _____
17 He hopes to finish it completely by the weekend. _____
18 The work has already been completed. _____

Exercise 232 Ask a question about the underlined part of each sentence. Use <u>what</u>, <u>who</u>, <u>how</u>, etc.

1 It was taken <u>yesterday</u>. _____ *When was it taken?*
2 The box will be delivered <u>by messenger</u>. _____
3 We were assisted by <u>several people</u>. _____
4 This has been known <u>for a long time</u>. _____
5 That is usually done <u>by this method</u>. _____
6 We'll learn it <u>by practicing a great deal</u>. _____
7 The report was prepared by <u>the two men</u>. _____
8 It was done <u>because it was necessary</u>. _____
9 <u>More than twelve</u> houses have already been sold. _____
10 <u>Mr. Brown</u> was met by the members of the club. _____
11 It will be finished <u>by ten-thirty or eleven o'clock</u>. _____
12 <u>Some important information</u> was presented by them. _
13 <u>By working hard</u>, they earned enough money. _____
14 That fact has been mentioned <u>several times</u> before. _
15 She promised <u>to give us an answer soon</u>. _____
16 Several members objected to <u>using that method</u>. _____
17 The woman turned around <u>to see it better</u>. _____
18 The president sent his answer to <u>Wilson</u>. _____
19 It was sent <u>by registered mail</u>. _____
20 <u>The first two</u> of them have already been returned. _____

Exercise 233 Change these statements to negatives.

1 It was broken by them. _____ *It wasn't broken by them.*
2 Art still likes to play football. _____
3 That class will be taught by Mr. Wilson. _____
4 He bought some new shoes yesterday. _____
5 I have no money right now. _____
6 Mr. Smith also enjoys baseball. _____
7 The house has already been painted. _____
8 I felt quite well this morning. _____
9 She enjoys watching certain television programs. _____
10 There were a few people in the room. _____
11 I have never eaten at that restaurant. _____
12 Then we'll expect to see you after class. _____
13 That work has already been completed. _____
14 He has some money now. _____
15 The people have already left for home. _____
16 We planned to leave on Saturday too. _____
17 Tom has always been a good student. _____
18 There have been some bad storms recently. _____

Exercise 234   Use only <u>in</u>, <u>on</u>, or <u>at</u>.

1   They go to the ballet ____occasion.
2   We went ____spite of the weather.
3   When did they arrive ____the hotel?
4   It's not interesting. ____the contrary, it's dull.
5   They insisted ____an immediate answer.
6   Why are you mad ____me?
7   Close that door ____once!
8   ____ all, there were twenty-two guests.
9   We didn't care for it ____the least.
10   Do you usually get to work ____time?
11   ____best, we will finish it by Thursday.
12   Why are you ____such a hurry?
13   He glanced ____his watch quickly.
14   ____general, this one is much easier.
15   When do you expect to arrive ____Detroit?
16   All ____all, we had a wonderful time.
17   Do you expect to live ____that salary?
18   They live ____the tenth floor of that building.
19   Does she plan to stay ____the Washington Hotel?
20   Is the car parked ____front of the house?
21   He's working ____a book about Lincoln.
22   He's always tired ____the end of the day.
23   Tom usually sits ____back of me.
24   Did he do that ____purpose?
25   ____my opinion, that's the wrong answer.
26   I'm more interested ____history than English.
27   ____the whole, we've learned a great deal.
28   They are laughing ____his funny answer.
29   We'll wait right here ____the meantime.
30   ____present, we're doing the last lesson.
31   She always depends ____them for help with it.
32   ____second thought, I'll do the work for you.
33   The man looked ____the list carefully.
34   They plan to be back ____a very short time.
35   He gave a good lecture ____that subject.
36   Tom is good ____remembering people's names.
37   ____first, this course seemed quite easy.
38   ____a few weeks, it seemed much harder
39   Now we're ____the last page of the book.
40   Well, we've finished this book ____last!

THE END!

202

VOCABULARY FOR LESSON SEVENTEEN

Pages 193 - 202

admit 195
advise 197
amount 199
announce 197
approve 196
Art 201
avoid 195
ballet 202
behave 199
behave 199
bore 199
Brazilian 200
breeze 198
cancel 197
careless 199
carpenter 197
clear 200
consider 195
constantly 200
construct 197
continue 196
cover 195
criticize 199
criticism 196
damage 199
delay 197
demand 199
dentist 200
deny 195
despise 196
discover 199
dull 202
expect 194
fact 201
firm 197
fog 198
frighten 198

hope 194
hurry 199
idea 200
increase 199
injure 197
inspect 199
intend 194
interrupt 199
join 199
knowledge 199
list 202
machinery 199
manage 197
messenger 198
official 199
permit 199
plan 194
postpone 195
president 197
quarrel 199
reduce 199
registered 201
repair 199
sleeve 200
spoil 197
storm 201
swim 196
thieves 198
toe 195
trust 198
warn 199
wealthy 196
wish 194

Bert, I've forgotten something important. I'm trying to remember it.

Think hard, Harry. It'll come to you.

Bert! I've got it! I remember now.

That's fine, Harry, but you're choking me!

I want to tell all of the students in our class that this is the last lesson.

Of course, Harry. A wonderful idea. They'll all be happy.

APPENDIX

A1　The cardinal numbers

1	one	11	eleven	21	twenty-one
2	two	12	twelve	22	twenty-two
3	three	13	thirteen	30	thirty
4	four	14	fourteen	40	forty
5	five	15	fifteen	50	fifty
6	six	16	sixteen	60	sixty
7	seven	17	seventeen	70	seventy
8	eight	18	eighteen	80	eighty
9	nine	19	nineteen	90	ninety
10	ten	20	twenty	100	one hundred
					a hundred

200	two hundred	10,000	ten thousand
1000	one thousand	100,000	one hundred thousand
2000	two thousand	1,000,000	one million

A2　The ordinal numbers

1st	first	11th	eleventh	21st	twenty-first
2nd	second	12th	twelfth	22nd	twenty-second
3rd	third	13th	thirteenth	30th	thirtieth
4th	fourth	14th	fourteenth	40th	fortieth
5th	fifth	15th	fifteenth	50th	fiftieth
6th	sixth	16th	sixteenth	60th	sixtieth
7th	seventh	17th	seventeenth	70th	seventieth
8th	eighth	18th	eighteenth	80th	eightieth
9th	ninth	19th	nineteenth	90th	ninetieth
10th	tenth	20th	twentieth	100th	one hundredth
					a hundredth

English measurements ——— L I N E A R ——— metric equivalents

English		metric equivalents	
.3937	inch	= 1	centimeter
1.	inch	= 2.54	centimeters
1.	foot (12 inches)	= 30.48	centimeters
1.	yard (3 feet)	= .9144	meter
3.2808	feet	= 1.	meter
3280.8	feet	= 1.	kilometer
5280.	feet (1 mile U.S.)	= 1.6	kilometers

——————————— L I Q U I D ———————————

1.	pint	= .473	liter
1.	quart (2 pints)	= .9463	liter
2.1134	pints	= 1.	liter
1.	gallon U.S. (4 quarts)	= 3.7853	liters

——————————— D R Y ———————————

.035	ounce	= 1.	gram
1.	ounce	= 28.3495	grams
1.	pound (16 ounces)	= .4536	kilogram
2.205	pounds	= 1.	kilogram
2000.	pounds (1 ton)	= 907.18	kilograms
1.102	tons	= 1.	metric ton

——————————— ABBREVIATIONS ———————————

in. (")	=	inch	lb.	=	pound
ft. (')	=	foot, feet	t.	=	ton
yd.	=	yard	pt.	=	pint
mi.	=	mile	qt.	=	quart
oz.	=	ounce	gal.	=	gallon

205

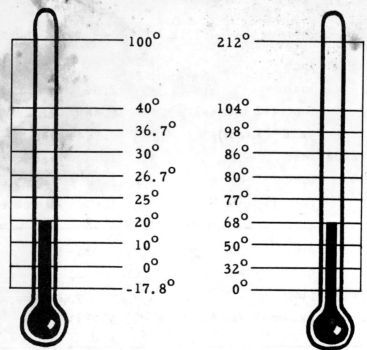

CENTIGRADE ➡ FAHRENHEIT

Multiply the Centigrade temperature by $\frac{9}{5}$.
Add 32 degrees to this.

FAHRENHEIT ➡ CENTIGRADE

Subtract 32 degrees from the Fahrenheit temperature.
Multiply by $\frac{5}{9}$.

95° F.   ninety-five degrees Fahrenheit
          ninety-five degrees
          ninety-five

15.5° C. fifteen and five-tenths degrees Centigrade
          fifteen and a half degrees Centigrade
          fifteen and a half
          fifteen point five

A5 The seasons and months of the year

spring	summer	fall	winter
March	June	September	December
April	July	October	January
May	August	November	February

A6 The days of the week

Sunday	Tuesday	Thursday	Saturday
Monday	Wednesday	Friday	

A7 Abbreviations: months and days

Mar.	=	March	Sun.	=	Sunday
Aug.	=	August	Mon.	=	Monday
Sept.	=	September	Tues.	=	Tuesday
Oct.	=	October	Wed.	=	Wednesday
Nov.	=	November	Thurs.	=	Thursday
Dec.	=	December	Fri.	=	Friday
Jan.	=	January	Sat.	=	Saturday
Feb.	=	February			

A8 The United States — *1950 Census*

the ten largest states

New York	14,830,192
California	10,586,223
Pennsylvania	10,498,012
Illinois	8,712,176
Ohio	7,946,627
Texas	7,711,194
Michigan	6,371,766
New Jersey	4,835,329
Massachusetts	4,690,514
North Carolina	4,061,929

the ten largest cities

(outside areas not included)

New York, N.Y.	7,835,099
Chicago, Ill.	3,606,436
Philadelphia, Pa.	2,064,794
Los Angeles, Cal.	1,957,692
Detroit, Mich.	1,838,517
Baltimore, Md.	940,205
Cleveland, Ohio	905,636
St. Louis, Mo.	852,623
Washington, D.C.	797,670
Boston, Mass.	790,863

SUMMARY VOCABULARY LIST

a 1
ability 15
about 3
above 11
absent 6
absolutely 14
accent 14
accept 10
accident 11
accidentally 15
according 15
accustomed 14
across 11
action 9
Adams 7
add 6
address 1
admire 14
admit 17
advertisement 11
advertising 7
advice 12
advise 17
afraid 10
Africa 12
after 6
afternoon 2
afterwards 6
again 11
against 9
agent 10
ago 6
agree 5
agriculture 14
air 9
airmail 7
airplane 3
airport 9
Alaska 13
Alice 5
all 4
almost 9
along 10
alongside 15
already 12
also 13
always 5
am 1
A. M. 5
ambitious 16

American 1
amount 17
an 1
and
angrily 11
announce 17
another 7
answer 2
any 5
anything 12
apartment 1
apple 1
application 9
apply 15
appointment 13
approve 17
April 9
are 1
area 15
aren't 1
Argentina 9
argue 15
argument 8
Arizona 13
arm 10
army 10
around 8
arrive 6
art 10
Art 17
article 8
artist 13
as 15
ash 10
ashtray 2
ask 2
assignment 6
assist 10
assistance 13
associate 14
at 3
ate 7
attempt 12
attend 4
attractive 16
August 5
aunt 6
author 13
automobile 2
autumn 15

avenue 7
average 15
avoid 17
away 4
awkward 16
baby 1
back 7
bad 2
bald 14
ball 3
ballet 17
ballpoint pen 5
bank 4
baseball 4
basement 11
bat 6
bathroom 3
Baton Rouge 16
be 4
beach 10
beautiful 2
because 11
become 8
bedroom 3
been 12
before 6
began 8
begin 3
begun 12
behave 17
behavior 14
Belgium 14
belong 6
believe 15
beside 7
besides 15
best 15
bet 8
better 15
Betty 5
between 8
bicycle 11
big 1
Bill 7
bill 4
billfold 7
bird 15
birth 13
birthday 7
bit 8

bite 8
black 14
blank 9
blackboard 3
blew 8
block 6
blond 15
blouse 2
blow 8
blown 12
blue 10
boat 4
Bob 11
body 1
bone 4
book 1
bookcase 13
bore 17
born 13
borrow 6
boss 11
Boston 7
both 9
bottle 5
boulevard 7
bowl 15
box 1
boy 1
bracelet 13
Brazil 2
Brazilian 17
bread 5
break 8
breakfast 3
breeze 17
bridge 11
briefcase 8
briefly 15
bright 16
brilliant 16
bring 7
Broadway 7
broke 8
broken 12
Brooklyn 11
brother 7
brought 7
brown 11
Brown 1
build 7

building 3
built 7
burn 10
bus 3
business 8
busy 1
but 4
butter 5
buy 2
cabinet 11
cafeteria 5
cage 15
cake 5
California 4
call 4
calm 16
camera 3
can 11
Canada 5
cancel 17
candidate 15
candle 13
candy 2
capital 15
car 1
care 14
careful 8
carefully 3
careless 17
carpenter 17
carry 3
cartoon 16
cat 11
catalog 11
catch 8
Catholic 15
caught 8
celebration 6
cents 11
cereal 8
certain 14
chair 2
change 9
chapter 3
Charles 2
charming 16
cheap 3
check 4
chemistry 14
Chicago 8
child 1

children 1
Chile 6
chilly 15
China 2
Chinese 6
chocolate 14
choice 11
choose 7
chose 7
chosen 12
Christmas 13
church 1
cigar 2
cigarette 2
citizen 8
city 4
class 1
classical 14
classroom 4
clean 10
clear 17
clerk 3
climate 14
clinic 13
clock 11
closet 6
cloth 12
clothes 6
cloudy 12
club 9
clumsy 16
coast 15
coat 1
coffee 2
cold 1
the Coliseum 12
collar 15
collect 9
college 8
Colombia 6
colonial 15
color 11
Colorado 10
combine 15
come 2
comfortable 4
common 11
company 6
compare 15
compensate 15
complain 15

complete 10
completely 15
complicated 16
conceited 16
concert 4
conference 14
confident 16
consider 17
considerate 16
consist 14
constantly 17
construct 17
contest 10
continue 17
contrary 14
cook 8
cool 6
copy 12
corner 5
correctly 5
cost 8
Costa Rica 13
cotton 6
couch 14
cough 11
count 3
country 6
course 4
court 14
cousin 10
cover 17
crazy 11
cream 5
credit 14
criticize 17
criticism 17
crowd 8
cry 2
Cuba 4
Cuban 5
cup 7
cupboard 11
curious 16
custom 9
cut 8
cute 6
Dallas 9
damage 17
dance 4
dark 10
date 14

daughter 8
dawn 9
day 2
dead 12
decide 9
decorate 9
decoration 9
deep 16
defect 12
delay 17
delicious 1
deliver 9
demand 17
dentist 17
Denver 10
deny 17
depart 10
department
 store 11
depend 13
description 9
deserve 14
desk 2
despise 17
dessert 5
destroy 7
details 14
Detroit 8
diamond 13
dictionary 5
did 7
didn't 6
difference 14
different 8
difficult 1
difficulty 10
dime 2
dinner 4
direction 6
directions 12
director 16
discover 17
discuss 12
dish 1
divide 10
do 2
doctor 1
does 2
doesn't 2
dog 4
dollar 5

done 12
don't 2
door 3
dormitory 15
down 8
downtown 6
dozen 8
drank 7
drawer 2
dream 15
dress 1
drive 5
driven 12
driveway 7
drove 7
drugstore 8
drunk 12
dry 16
dull 17
during 5
Dutch 9
each 4
early 4
earn 13
earrings 13
easily 15
east 7
easy 1
easy chair 5
eat 3
eaten 12
economics 14
Ecuador 14
Ed 10
Edward 7
effort 14
egg 1
the Eiffel Tower 13
eight 4
eighteen 7
eighty 8
either 13
elect 11
election 8
electric 11
elementary 12
elevator 11
Elizabeth 4
else 13
embarrass 15
emergency 13

employ 14
empty 6
end 10
energetic 16
energy 12
England 2
English 1
enjoy 4
enough 5
enroll 13
entertainment 13
eraser 2
etc. 10
Europe 1
European 14
evening 8
ever 5
every 2
everybody 14
everyone 10
everything 14
exact 13
example 4
except 14
excited 15
exciting 15
exercise 3
exhibition 10
expect 17
expensive 3
experience 14
explain 6
export 15
fact 17
factory 11
fall 5
fallen 12
familiar 6
family 1
famous 14
far 11
farm 6
farther 15
farthest 15
fast 2
fat 5
father 8
Faulkner,Wm. 13
favorite 13
feature 12
February 9

federal 15
feet 1
fell 8
fellow 16
felt 7
fence 14
a few 5
fifth 7
fifty 7
film 3
finally 12
find 7
fine 11
finish 4
fire 6
fire department 9
fire extinguisher 9
fireplace 15
firm 17
first 8
fish 1
fit 8
five 7
fix 2
flat 15
flew 7
floor 2
Florida 4
flower 2
flown 12
fly 2
fog 17
follow 12
fond 14
food 5
foolish 16
foot 1
football 6
foreign 13
forever 10
forget 8
forgot 8
forgotten 12
formal 16
formerly 15
forty 11
Foster 13
found 7
fourteen 11
fourteenth 14
frame 15

free 13
French 2
frequently 5
Friday 9
friend 2
friendly 16
frighten 17
from 1
front 2
fruit 5
full 6
funny 4
furnace 11
furnish 14
furniture 5
further 15
furthest 15
gabardine 15
game 3
garage 7
Garcia 14
garden 2
gave 7
generous 16
Genoa 13
genuine 15
George 4
Germany 3
gift 7
girl 1
give 3
given 12
glance 15
glass 4
gloves 11
go 2
gold 13
golf 15
gone 12
good 1
good looking 2
got 8
gotten 12
grade 15
graduate 13
graduation 15
Grand Central
    Station 9
grandfather 15
grandmother 14
gray 9

great 6
Greece 9
Greek 14
green 2
grew 7
groceries 7
grocery store 4
group 10
grow 7
grown 12
guest 5
had 8
hair 11
half 8
hall 10
ham 10
handkerchief 5
handle 15
handsome 1
happen 11
happy 2
harbor 11
hard 2
hardware 11
Harry 13
has 2
hasn't 12
hat 2
hate 7
Havana 9
have 2
haven't 12
Hawaii 11
he 1
head 15
hear 3
heard 7
heavy 1
held 8
Helen 1
help 5
helpful 12
her 5
here 1
hers 8
he's 1
hid 8
hidden 12
hide 8
high 11
high heel shoes 9

high school 14
hill 11
him 5
historical 9
history 4
hit 3
hold 3
holiday 9
home 4
homely 16
hometown 9
homework 8
hope 17
hospital 3
hot 1
hot dog 14
hotel 6
hour 7
house 1
housecoat 11
however 12
how's 11
hundred 11
hungry 2
hurry 17
husband 10
I 1
ice 10
ice cream 5
idea 17
I'm 1
immediately 4
impolite 9
important 5
impressive 15
improve 12
in 1
increase 17
inch 9
information 12
initial 13
injure 17
insane 15
insist 14
inspect 17
instructions 10
instructor 3
intend 17
intentional 7
interested 14
interesting 1

interrupt 17
intersection 12
interview 15
introduce 7
into 3
invitation 9
invite 6
irregular 7
is 1
isn't 1
it 1
Italian 3
Italy 2
item 16
its 8
it's 1
I've 12
Jack 10
Jane 10
January 11
Japan 1
Japanese 7
Jefferson 15
jewelry 15
Jim 10
John 1
Johnson 9
join 17
joke 4
Jones 16
juice 14
jump 9
June 5
keep 5
kept 8
keys 13
kind 11
kitchen 5
knew 7
know 2
knowledge 17
known 12
Labor Day 14
lace 12
lady 1
land 9
language 1
large 3
last 6
late 4
later 8

Latin 14
laugh 4
law 14
lawyer 3
lazy 16
lead 8
learn 2
least 13
leather 9
leave 4
lecture 6
led 8
left 5
leg 8
lemon 11
lend 7
lens 15
lent 8
less 15
lesson 2
let's 4
letter 2
liberal 16
library 3
light 4
like 4
Lincoln 3
line 10
list 9
listen 3
a little 5
live 2
living room 10
loaf 11
loan 15
lock 9
London 13
long 3
Long Island 7
look 3
loose 15
Los Angeles 9
lose 8
lost 8
a lot of 5
lots of 5
loud 13
loudly 10
Louisiana 8
love 7
the Louvre 12

lovely 15
low 7
luck 12
lunch 6
machine 11
machinery 17
mad 8
made 8
maid 4
mail 7
mailman 8
main 6
make 4
man 1
manage 17
manners 14
many 2
map 3
March 9
mark 15
marry 16
Martha 6
Mary 1
match 3
matter 13
may 11
maybe 7
mayor 10
me 5
meal 7
meaning 8
meat 6
medical 14
meet 8
meeting 6
melt 14
member 9
memorize 14
men 1
mention 11
message 12
messenger 17
met 8
metal 15
method 15
Mexico 3
Miami 6
Michigan 8
midnight 9
the Midwest 11
mile 11

milk 2
mine 8
minute 6
mirror 4
Miss 2
miss 2
mistake 7
modern 15
moment 6
Monday 6
money 2
more 3
morning 4
Moscow 15
most 15
mother 5
motor 12
month 4
mountain 11
move 4
movie 3
Mr. 1
Mrs. 1
much 2
museum 7
music 3
my 8
nail 9
name 5
narrow 16
national 14
native language 15
navy 9
near 6
neat 16
necessary 10
necklace 13
need 2
nephew 8
nervous 16
never 5
new 1
news 2
newspaper 3
New York 2
next 4
nice 1
nickel 2
nickname 11
niece 8
night 5

nine 8
ninety 11
noise 3
noon 8
normal 16
north 7
Norway 10
notebook 3
nothing 11
notice 6
novel 9
November 11
now 1
number 6
nurse 3
object 15
obvious 12
occasionally 5
ocean 15
o'clock 5
October 11
offer 8
office 5
official 17
often 4
Ohio 7
oil 11
old 2
old-fashioned 12
on 2
once 4
one 1
only 3
open 3
opera 9
opportunity 14
or 6
orange 1
order 11
Oregon 10
organization 9
ornate 15
other 3
our 8
ours 8
out of 11
outside 6
over 7
overcoat 3
overshoes 10
owe 4

own 6
the Pacific 15
package 3
page 1
paid 8
pail 14
paint 11
painting 5
pair 7
pan 13
paper 4
parade 11
parents 10
Paris 12
part 10
past 12
Pat 12
patient 16
pay 4
paycheck 15
peculiar 15
pen 2
pencil 2
Pennsylvania 7
penny 2
people 2
pepper 5
per 11
perfect 12
period 9
permit 17
Persian 5
person 16
Peru 14
phone 10
photograph 2
physics 14
piano 4
picnic 12
picture 2
piece 7
pile 13
pint 14
place 12
plain 17
plan 9
plane 6
plastic 15
plate 5
play 3
player 16

pleasant 9
please 4
pleased 15
pleasure 15
plenty 14
pocket 8
pocketbook 7
poem 9
poker 15
policeman 10
police 14
polite 15
poor 13
popular 10
Portuguese 2
position 14
possible 15
post office 14
postpone 17
pot 13
pound 11
practical 14
practice 5
prediction 11
prefer 11
prepare 4
prepared 15
present 7
president 17
pretty 1
previous 8
price 7
prize 10
probably 7
professional 13
professor 9
profit 12
program 7
project 16
promise 13
prompt 15
pronounce 3
pronunciation 13
proper 13
properly 13
protect 15
proud 15
prove 7
proverb 14
purse 7
put 3

quarrel 17
quart 11
question 2
quickly 6
quiet 8
quit 8
quite 1
radio 1
rain 3
raincoat 10
Ralph 4
ran 8
rapidly 14
razor blade 8
reach 12
read 3
ready 1
really 9
receive 3
recently 15
recognize 11
record 14
recover 15
red 1
reduce 17
refrigerator 5
registered 17
regular 13
relative 8
rely 15
remain 10
remark 11
remember 6
remind 9
repair 17
repeat 3
reply 2
report 7
request 15
reserved 16
respect 13
respectful 16
restaurant 6
result 15
return 7
review 7
ridden 12
ride 7
ridiculous 11
right 5
ring 15

river 11
road 5
Robert 8
robin 11
rode 7
Rome 12
room 1
rope 11
round 8
row 12
rubber 15
rude 16
rug 2
ruin 9
run 8
Russian 13
safe 15
said 7
salary 14
sale 13
salt 5
same 5
sandwich 4
San Francisco 4
sang 7
sat 8
satisfied 15
Saturday 3
saw 7
say 5
school 3
scratch 12
season 6
seat 8
Seattle 10
second 7
secretary 12
section 14
select 15
selfish 16
sensible 16
sent 7
see 3
seem 2
seen 12
seldom 5
sell 6
semester 3
send 3
sentence 4
September 10

serious 12
set 9
seven 3
seventeenth 11
seventh 9
seventy 11
several 3
shade 11
shape 15
share 13
sharp 9
she 1
shelf 4
shelves 13
she's 1
shine 3
ship 11
shirt 2
shoes 2
short 5
shortly 14
shop 3
show 7
shut 3
sick 1
side 4
sidewalk 7
sight 15
sign 6
silk 12
silver 15
similar 4
simple 14
since 12
sincere 16
sing 7
sister 8
sit 3
situation 10
sixteen 8
size 16
skirt 7
sleep 3
sleepy 6
sleeve 17
slept 7
slid 8
slide 8
slip 6
slippery 14
slow 16

slowly 6
sly 11
small 1
smart 2
smell 3
smile 3
Smith 1
smoke 4
smooth 6
snow 3
so 11
soccer 10
sociable 16
socks 4
soft 15
sold 7
soldier 11
solution 14
some 3
someone 4
something 9
sometimes 5
son 7
song 5
soon 11
sometime 10
sometimes 10
sorry 13
sort 11
sound 14
soup 6
South America 1
the Soviet Union 15
Spain 2
Spanish 2
sparrow 11
speak 2
special delivery 9
speech 14
spell 3
spend 2
spent 7
spin 8
spoil 17
spoke 7
spoken 12
spoon 6
sport 13
sport coat 13
sports 10
spot 14

spread 8
spring 6
spun 8
square 14
stamp 14
stand 8
start 3
state 8
statement 14
statue 14
stay 9
steak 9
steal 8
steel 15
steps 8
Stevens 6
still 13
St. Louis 10
stockings 11
stole 8
stolen 12
stone 14
stood 8
stop 3
stop light 11
store 2
storm 17
story 1
stove 11
straight 5
strange 16
street 6
strict 14
stripe 11
strong 4
student 1
study 2
stupid 16
substitute 13
subject 14
suburban 14
subway 6
sugar 4
suggest 7
suggestion 11
suit 2
suitcase 4
summer 5
sun 1
Sunday 6
sunrise 9

sunset 9
super market 10
supplies 14
sure 11
surprise 6
suspenders 10
suspicious 14
sweater 6
sweet 16
sweetheart 16
swim 17
symphony 14
table 2
tactful 16
take 7
taken 12
tall 1
taught 7
tea 4
teach 2
teacher 1
team 8
tear 8
teeth 1
telegram 13
telephone 3
television 3
tell 7
ten 4
tennis 14
tennis court 12
tenth 9
terrible 14
test 7
Texas 9
textbook 14
thank 12
that 2
that's 2
the 1
theater 11
their 8
theirs 8
them 5
then 8
therefore 12
there's 3
these 2
they 1
they're 1
they've 12

thick 16
thief 9
thieves 17
thin 14
thing 5
think 3
third 9
thirsty 5
thirty 11
this 2
those 2
thoughtful 16
thousand 4
three 2
threw 8
throw 7
thrown 12
ticket 7
tie 10
time 5
times 5
tiny 15
tired 1
title 8
toast 5
toaster 11
today 1
toe 17
together 8
told 7
Tom 3
tomorrow 9
tonight 9
too 5
took 7
tool 11
tooth 1
top 9
topcoat 9
tore 8
torn 12
tough 10
tourist 13
tournament 16
towel 3
toy 2
traffic 6
train 7
translate 9
travel 4
tree 4

trip 6
trouble 8
true 5
trust 17
try 2
Tuesday 6
turn 11
twelve 7
twenty 11
twice 13
two 1
type 16
typewriter 6
umbrella 3
uncle 4
under 11
understand 2
understood 8
the United States 1
university 6
until 8
unusual 14
us 5
use 6
usually 4
vacation 6
valuable 14
vegetable 9
Venezuela 7
ventilation 14
verb 6
Vermont 15
very 1
violin 14
visit 3
visitor 6
vocabulary 13
wait 8
wall 2
want 3
war 14
warm 5
warn 17
was 6
wash 2
Washington 7
wasn't 6
wastebasket 3
watch 3
water 4
way 16

we 1
weak 5
wealthy 17
wear 4
weather 1
wedding 14
Wednesday 15
week 3
weekend 11
well 2
went 7
we're 1
were 6
weren't 6
west 15
we've 12
what 3
what's 3
wheel 8
when 11
when's 11
where 11
where's 11
which 11
while 10
white 1
White 7
who 11
whole 16
whom 11
who's 11
whose 11
why 11
wide 5
wife 9
Williams 3
win 8
wind 8
window 2
winter 6
wish 16
within 11
without 15
woman 1
women 1
won 8
wonderful 9
won't 9
wood 16
wool 15
word 1

wore 7
work 2
worker 11
world 14
the World Series 14
worn 12
worry 14
worse 15
worst 15
would 4
write 2
writer 13
written 12
wrong 6
wrote 7
year 4
yellow 2
yesterday 6
yet 1
you 1
young 4
your 8
you're 1
yours 8
you've 12